BULLY NATION

Why America's Approach to Childhood Aggression is Bad for Everyone

BULLY NATION

Why America's Approach to Childhood Aggression is Bad for Everyone

Susan Eva Porter, Ph.D., LCSW., M.S.Ed.

PARAGON HOUSE

First Edition 2013

Published in the United States by

Paragon House
1925 Oakcrest Ave, Suite 7
St. Paul, MN 55113
www.ParagonHouse.com

Library of Congress Cataloging-in-Publication Data

Porter, Susan Eva, 1963-
Bully nation : why America's approach to childhood aggression is bad for everyone / Susan Eva Porter. -- 1st ed.
    p. cm.
Summary: "Looks at how assigning labels like 'bully' and 'victim' inhibits childhood development in the name of keeping kids safe. The book reviews normal child development, the role of aggression in a healthy childhood, how children develop resilience, and provides strategies for social policy related to bullying"--Provided by publisher.
ISBN 978-1-55778-904-4 (pbk. : alk. paper) 1. Bullying in schools--United States. 2. Bullying in schools--United States--Prevention. 3. Problem children--Behavior modification--United States. 4. Agression in children--United States. 5. Child psychology--United States. I. Title.
LB3013.32.P67 2013
371.5'8--dc23

                    2012034216

The paper used in this publication meets the minimum requirements of American National Standard for Information Sciences— Permanence of Paper for Printed Library Materials, ANSIZ39.48-1984.

Manufactured in the United States of America
10 9 8 7 6 5 4 3 2 1

For current information about all releases from Paragon House, visit the website at http://www.ParagonHouse.com

To my students,
past, present, and future,
who provide me with inspiration every day

Acknowledgements

I spend most of my time hanging out with educators, who, by and large, are a pretty amazing group of people. In fact, if you're not a teacher, and if you can't stand the people you work with, then I suggest you go into teaching. It won't be easy, but if you become a teacher you will be surrounded by the most earnest, hard-working, and dedicated professionals in the world, I guarantee it. My colleagues inspire all of my writing in one way or another; the conversations I have with them, the observations I make of them, and the lessons I learn from them all conspire to point me in the right direction.

Some colleagues in particular have made this book possible, either directly or indirectly. First and foremost, I'd like to thank Steve Morris, Julie Galles, and Maggie Weis (Lady Cop) of The San Francisco School for their support, professionalism, and senses of humor. You are simply incredible, and I couldn't have written this book without your helpful insights, encouragement, and friendship. I will miss you, and thanks.

Second, thanks to Lochlann Jain, Associate Professor of Anthropology, Stanford University, and my sister Jessica Porter, for that conversation at Thanksgiving. I needed the nudge.

Third, thanks to Lise Shelton, Dean of Faculty at The Bay School of San Francisco, for letting me bounce off ideas.

Finally, thanks to my agent, Bertram Linder, of Educational Design Services, for helping me twice.

CONTENTS

INTRODUCTION

America's Got a Problem with Bullying

I just Googled "bullying statistics," and this is what popped up:

- 1 in 5 children is bullied.
- 23% of students say they been bullied several times.
- 1 in 4 children is bullied.
- 50% of children are bullied, and 10% are bullied on a regular basis.
- 74% of 8- to 11-year-olds said teasing and bullying occurs at their schools.
- 77% of students say they've been bullied recently.
- It is estimated that more than half of school bullying incidents are never reported.

Besides the fact that these statistics are wildly inconsistent, they suggest America has a real problem with childhood aggression, and that bullying is everywhere. You already know this if you're a parent or a teacher. If you're a parent, perhaps your own child has been bullied, or maybe someone has accused your child of being a bully or a "mean girl." If you're a teacher, perhaps you've had to deal with children who are bullying or being bullied, or you've been trained about your school's Anti-Bullying policies and instructed about how to respond to bullying.

Even if bullying hasn't affected you personally, you know it's a problem because, statistics aside, everyone is talking about it. If you missed your local school or community center's symposium on bullying, then perhaps you saw the webcast hosted by President and Mrs. Obama on the subject. Or you've heard horror stories at a recent PTA meeting. Or you've simply been paying attention. Unless you've been media-free for the past few years, you've been exposed to bully news in newspapers, on TV, and all over the Internet. In fact, the topic of bullying has made its way into pop culture like no other issue facing kids today. Indeed, other topics that affect our children—such as smoking, drunk driving, or school funding—haven't made it onto the cover of People magazine, but bullying has. Bullying is an attention grabber, and it has America's attention.

This makes sense. We should pay attention when our kids get hurt, either physically or psychologically; it's imperative that we respond. However, as a counselor with over 20 years experience working in schools with teenagers, children, and their parents, I have come to believe that many of our current responses to the bullying "epidemic" are deeply flawed, regardless of our good intentions. In our desire to help kids feel safe, and fueled by our fears about the startling bully statistics, we have developed methods of responding to childhood aggression that often do more harm than good.

For instance, some of our responses to bullying send kids the message that they shouldn't have to tolerate even the mildest forms of emotional pain or social discomfort, and that such discomfort is inherently bad and possibly dangerous to their long-term emotional well being. Others send the message that parents and teachers should play an active, even aggressive, role in mediating the social lives of children, and that kids don't have the resources to solve problems on their own. Still others pit kids against one another in ways that make it difficult for them ever to fully resolve their issues. As a result, rather than fostering resilience in kids, much of what we do now leaves them feeling disempowered and stigmatized, and leaves the adults around them feeling helpless and frustrated.

In making the claim that our approaches to bullying are flawed, I am not suggesting that kids can't be mean, thoughtless, and even violent at times, and feel miserable as a result. Children can be downright nasty to each other, and they can suffer terribly in their relationships with their peers. I am also not suggesting that children don't need our guidance when it comes to their behavior. They do. They definitely need our help. But as I will explain throughout this book, the help we're giving them when it comes to bullying also causes problems, and we need to reexamine our own responses when it comes to our kids' behavior, if we wish to help them feel safe and develop lasting resilience.

So, yes, America's got a problem with bullying—a big problem—but there's much more to it than just the behavior between kids. The way we currently think about, measure, and understand aggressive behavior is also problematic. The above-cited statistics on bullying attest to the fact that we haven't solved the bully problem yet, and throughout this book I will explore why this has as much to do with how we approach the bully problem as it does with the behavior itself.

Three Reasons Why Our Approach to Bullying is Bad for Everyone

There are three main reasons why America's approach to bullying is bad for everyone, and I will explore each in depth in the following chapters. Any of these reasons, once you fully understand it, should be enough to convince you that our culture's attitude about childhood aggression is problematic. When you consider all three reasons together, however, I am certain you will come to see why our current efforts to keep our children safe and happy in their relationships with each other—while well-intended—are doing them more harm than good.

The first reason our approach to bullying is bad is that we're using ineffective and damning language to describe the situations that arise between kids. Language may not seem like such a big deal when kids are hurting one another, but it is. It's a huge deal because the words we use to describe situations between kids, and the labels we give kids, such as bully, victim, bystander and ally (to name a few), strip us of our power to help kids understand the dynamics between them. Language creates the frame through which we see and understand our world, and therefore it is vitally important that we be careful and considerate in our language when we're dealing with kids. Bully Language is limiting at best and damaging at worst.

Think about it. When was the last time you felt compassion for a bully? "Bully" labels distance us from the kids we're talking about, and they rob us of compassion for kids in need. When we stop having compassion for kids—even misbehaving kids—we're in trouble, and I will explain how our Bully Language encourages us to deal with many of our children without compassion and with a fixed, instead of a flexible, mindset. This fixed approach makes it difficult for us to question our methods or to think creatively as we respond to difficult situations between kids, and it fosters an Us vs. Them mentality when what we need to do is to work together to help kids learn from their mistakes and develop resilience in the face of pain.

Our language is important, and I will explore in Chapter 1 how the labels and mindset we use to describe our childhood aggression don't serve them or us.

The second reason our approach to bullying is bad for everyone is because, in our desire to protect kids from emotional pain, we have expanded the definition to include almost any behavior that has the potential to make a child feel bad. Being unfriendly, social exclusion, and name-calling are just a few of the behaviors that have recently inched their way into the bully ring.

To define these behaviors as bullying is to swell the original definition almost beyond recognition, and with our acceptance of such behaviors as bullying, our children are now instructed to be on high alert for all manner of social slights. Many children are taught that when they feel any kind of emotional pain at the hands of another, then they've been bullied, and thus seriously wounded. Children now toss around the term bullying freely—as do many of their parents—and this is a direct result of this expanded definition of the term.

Most states and school districts have taken this swollen definition and instituted policies that call us into action when a child feels hurt on a range of accounts and, once a child says she's been bullied, these policies often require that we proceed in a lockstep manner. Rather than helping kids, the mandated procedures we must follow can discourage the development of psychological resilience in kids. For example, an overkill response, which is common given the more recent, broader definition of bullying, teaches kids that someone else is to blame for their psychological distress, and that they may have suffered deep and lasting harm from their painful experiences. I have worked with kids who, once they've been identified as victims of bullying, become less able to self-advocate, or worse yet, more inclined when they feel distressed to locate responsibility for their feelings outside of themselves and point the finger at another.

The broader definition of bullying accounts for much of the supposed increase we are seeing in bullying behavior in our culture. Adults often ask me if kids today are worse than those of previous generations. My answer is an emphatic no. Kids haven't changed, but our definitions of their negative behaviors have, and this has had a profound effect on how they think about themselves and their relationships with their peers. This has also created a level of fear in our culture that is infectious. Parents especially are terrified of bullying, but sometimes they don't even know what they're afraid of. Ask parents if their child being excluded from a social event, or having a sustained period of difficulty with friends, is the end of the world, and they will reply no. Ask them if their child being bullied is the end of the world, and they will reply yes.

How we define bullying matters, and I will explain in Chapter 2 how our ballooning definition of bullying causes kids to feel victimized even when they haven't been.

The third and final reason our approach to bullying is bad for everyone is because, with the expanded definition of bullying, we expect kids to behave, and to learn from their behavior, in ways that are often well beyond their developmental capacities. You don't have to be a teacher to know that it takes time to learn reading, writing, and arithmetic, and yet, when it comes to social-emotional learning, we have an expectation that kids will "get it" right away. Our current approach to bullying, in the form of many of our state and school policies, is often one of Zero Tolerance.

Can you imagine what would happen if we had a Zero Tolerance approach to teaching kids math? This would be ridiculous—let alone terrible teaching—and we'd have a lot of failure on our hands. And yet, in our culture of fear of bullying, this is often how we deal with teaching kids about relationships, and instructing them on how not to be mean and nasty and thoughtless and careless with one another. And while these negative behaviors certainly demand our attention, we must remember that helping kids change in the social-emotional department takes as much time and thoughtful guidance as it does in any other aspect of their learning, and perhaps even more.

Note that kids do math for maybe an hour a day, and yet they must contend with their emotions, relationships, and with each other most of the time. It therefore makes sense that it would take us even longer to teach them how to behave well with each other, and to learn from their mistakes and move on, than to teach them a difficult subject such as algebra. And yet we set them up for failure with policies that demand they master their emotional and relational challenges immediately.

When we set standards and benchmarks for our children's behavior, we must keep in mind that the human brain does not reach maturity until about 25 years of age. Twenty-five! Expecting anything less than perfection from a 13-year-old brain is crazy on our part, and yet many of our Anti-Bullying policies set such unreasonable and unachievable expectations. I have dealt with plenty of nasty, horrible, and unbearable 13-year-olds who, with the benefit of time and gentle and loving guidance, turn into the nicest, kindest, most thoughtful 18-year-olds. It's called development, and kids need help with it, not to be labeled and stigmatized in the midst of it.

Development is important, and I will discuss in Chapter 3 how we must take emotional, social, and cognitive development into consideration when we set our expectations for childhood behavior.

Advancing the Conversation: Phase 2

It is time to deepen our understanding of the issue of aggression in childhood, to refine our best practices, and to loosen our grip on methods of responding that turn complicated and nuanced situations into simple, black-and-white scenarios. The work that has been done thus far to protect our children is praiseworthy, but it is incomplete. While we have expended significant effort to recognize what happens between kids, we have also inadvertently created a framework of responding that limits us in ways we never anticipated, and we are now at an impasse. Let's call this Phase 1.

In Phase 2, we evaluate what were doing, keep what works, discard what doesn't, and create new methods of thinking and responding where needed. We can become even more effective in our efforts to help kids navigate the stormy seas of childhood and adolescence by engaging in a conversation about what we're presently doing, not by just assuming that our current methods are adequate. During Phase 1, we created an awareness of the pains children suffer in their relationships. In Phase 2, we advance this awareness and further our efforts to help children thrive.

After examining why our approach to bullying is bad for everyone in Chapters 1 through 3, in Chapter 4 I will introduce the GRIT approach to dealing with childhood aggression. There are four steps to the GRIT approach. They are:

1. Growth Mindset

2. Responding versus Reacting

3. Interventions

4. Teaching

GRIT offers a different way to think about and deal with childhood aggression and ways of dealing with childhood aggression, a method that doesn't employ labels but instead promotes a growth mindset and fosters resilience. GRIT offers a way to move forward in our effort to help children, and it does so without vilifying them and making them the enemy.

A Note To The Reader

As I considered whether to write this book, I had to weigh my concerns that our accepted practices of managing childhood aggression sometimes cause more harm than good against respecting the status quo when it comes to dealing with bullying. Clearly, I made the decision to move forward with this work, and to offer my opinions, clinical observations, and suggestions about what's happening with kids today. In proceeding, I have no intention of criticizing individual people or organizations that promote Anti-Bullying policies or attitudes. Everyone I know who is tackling the "bully epidemic" is doing so with the noblest of intentions, and should be recognized for their efforts. To this end, I have no specific targets as I offer my critiques, just a desire to deconstruct and examine the bullying issue from various angles, with the hope that such an exercise can bring us closer to achieving our shared goal of keeping kids safe.

Before I dive in, I want to reiterate that kids can suffer deeply in their relationships with each other, and that we should always take their suffering seriously. In the following chapters, as I examine how we attend to this suffering, I may sound critical at times. And I am being critical, but never of the kids, even the ones who misbehave. That said, I am also not an apologist for bad behavior, and my criticisms of some of our methods of dealing with bullying should not be understood as such; I do not subscribe to the "boys will be boys" philosophy of childrearing.

Rather than taking aim at our kids, their parents, or teachers, my intention is to critique our conceptual frameworks about bullying because such a process of self-examination and self-reflection can help us serve children more effectively. Like everyone who fights against bullying, I want to help children avoid suffering, if possible, but more importantly—because all children will suffer at some point in their relationships with each other—I want to help children develop resilience and strength in the face of their suffering.

Please note that this book is about how we deal with children and adolescents and their aggression with each other. It's not about adult aggression or misbehavior. When I talk about children, I will often specify their ages, but where I don't, you may assume that the kids in question are no older than 17. The kinds of things I encourage us to do for children, such as have compassion for them when their brains misfire and they hurt others, or to be patient and understanding when they can't be these things with each other, I do not necessarily advocate when it comes to dealing with adults. My arguments within this book apply only to our attitudes about children, and my opinions should not be extrapolated to apply to adults who are aggressive with one another or with children.

Finally, throughout *Bully Nation* I use case material to illustrate concepts and elaborate on themes. When such material comes from the public domain, I have cited the source. When it doesn't, I have altered the information to protect the identity of those involved. In some instances, I have created amalgams in an effort to either clarify a point or protect the identity of those involved.

CHAPTER 1

THE PROBLEMS WITH BULLY LANGUAGE

BULLY LANGUAGE IS THE TERM I use to describe how many people in our culture talk about aggression between children. It's comprised of the labels given to children who are involved in bullying, and the words used to discuss negative actions among kids. Bully Language influences how we understand childhood aggression, and it also shapes and dictates our collective responses to it. This chapter explores ten specific problems that arise from the use of Bully Language and explains how they hinder us in our pursuit of keeping children truly healthy and safe.

The Case of Mary

Mary was an exuberant yet sensitive 12-year-old. She loved nothing more than to be around classmates and interact with peers. She was drawn to the "popular" girls in her class, and often sought them out at recess and after school. But despite Mary's desire to connect and make friends, she often had trouble in her relationships. She was picked on occasionally, and felt left out at times. Like most girls her age, she was very sensitive to her social standing and status, and it bothered her when she was having trouble with friends.

One day after school, Mary jumped into the car and exclaimed to her father, "Everyone hates me!" She then burst into tears and cried all the way home. Mary's father couldn't calm her down and when Mary remained upset through dinner, both her parents became concerned. Her mother went to Mary's room in an effort to console her.

"Tell me what happened," she said.

Mary explained to her mom that she had been excluded by a group of girls at lunch that day. When she'd approached their table to sit with them, the girls had told Mary there was no room for her. Mary said it was the third time that week she'd been excluded, and she didn't know how much more she could take. She also said she had received some disturbing e-mails from someone she considered to be a friend, who was one of the girls who had excluded her.

"It said 'I hate you,'" Mary confessed. She showed her mother the e-mail, plus others she had received in the past, some from as long as two years before.

The next day, Mary sobbed again when her father picked her up from school, and she reported that the same thing had happened at lunch that day.

"I don't want to go to school anymore," Mary declared. "I can't stand it!"

Mary's parents didn't know what to do. They had never seen their daughter react this way before. She seemed inconsolable. Her feelings of helplessness and sadness were palpable, and it wasn't long before Mary's parents felt helpless, too. They tried everything they could to help their daughter feel better about the situation, but nothing seemed to help. When she wasn't crying, Mary was glum and depressed, and she barely engaged in conversation. After a week of this, Mary's father could no longer tolerate his own feelings of anger at the girls who had done this to his daughter, so he made an appointment to see the vice principal at Mary's school.

"My daughter is being bullied," he reported, as he showed the vice principal the copies of the e-mails Mary had received. "Here's the proof."

While the vice principal reviewed the e-mails, Mary's father said, "I want to know what the school's going to do about all this bullying—this is unacceptable. I thought you had an Anti-Bullying policy."

Mary's father detailed the behavior his daughter was being subjected to at lunchtime each day, and he gave the vice principal a list of names of the girls involved. "My daughter doesn't want to come to school anymore because of this," he said. "I want you to take care of this immediately—I'm not going tolerate my daughter getting bullied anymore."

"Of course not," the vice principal responded sincerely.

"And I want to know what happens to these girls," Mary's father added. "I want to make sure they get properly punished."

The vice principal thanked Mary's father for bringing this to her attention and assured him that she would take care of the situation. According to the school's protocol, she was required to interview all the children involved and inform their parents about what was going on. Whenever a charge of bullying was made, the school had to proceed according to the protocol established by the school district, and every charge of bullying had to be investigated, documented, and reported to the superintendant.

The vice principal called the offending girls into her office separately.

"You have been accused of bullying," she told each one of them. "Can you tell me what happened?"

The girls had various reactions to the vice principal's question, from tears to defensiveness to disbelief. "What do you mean we bullied someone?" one of them asked.

"Is it true that you didn't let Mary sit at your table at lunch?" the vice principal asked.

"Sort of," the girl replied cautiously. "But there weren't enough seats," she explained.

"That's social exclusion," the vice principal explained, "and that's bullying. You can always find another chair."

"Yes, ma'am," the girl responded softly, fighting back the tears.

Another girl exclaimed, "But I didn't do anything! I wasn't the one who said Mary couldn't sit at our table."

"That means you were a bystander," the vice principal replied curtly. "Do you remember what we learned about bystanders during our Anti-Bullying workshop?" The girl looked at her tentatively, afraid to speak for fear of saying the wrong thing. When the girl didn't respond, the vice principal continued. "Bystanders are just as guilty as bullies," she explained. "It was your responsibility to help Mary during this situation. It's not enough for you to say you're not the bully—it's your job to do something."

"But I didn't know Mary was feeling bad," the girl said sheepishly.

"That's not the point," the vice principal replied. "You knew the other girls were doing something wrong. You must be an ally when bullying happens, not a bystander. Being an ally means it is your responsibility to stand up for the victim when you see bullying happening and to tell an adult immediately. Do you understand?" The girl nodded in agreement.

To the girl who wrote the e-mails to Mary, the vice principal said, "Can you explain to me why you wrote this?" She showed the girl copies of the e-mails. The girl blushed.

"Well?" the vice principal said. "Why did you say these things? What caused you to say such hateful things?"

"But Mary said bad things to me, too," the girl said defensively.

"I'm not interested in what Mary said. I'm interested in what you said, and in your actions," the vice principal replied.

"But I don't even remember writing this one," the girl responded, pointing to the oldest e-mail.

"So you admit you wrote the others, then?" the vice principal asked.

The girl searched for words. She was silent for a moment. "Mary can be annoying sometimes," the girl admitted, "Maybe I was mad at her when I sent them."

"Being mad at someone is no excuse for bullying," the vice principal replied, as she wrapped up the meeting.

After her conversations with each of the girls, during which the vice principal became convinced that Mary had been bullied through willful and repeated exclusion and harassing e-mails, she called the offending girls' parents to inform them what had happened.

"Your daughter is a member of a group that has been bullying a class-mate," she informed each parent. "There have been several troubling incidents of social exclusion and harassment, and they must stop. As her punishment, your daughter must write a letter of apology to the child involved, an essay on how to prevent bullying, and serve a detention after school. We will also be monitoring the lunchroom more closely to make sure this doesn't continue. Your daughter and her friends may be assigned seats at lunch if we don't see an effort to include others."

"This is outrageous!" one of the parents responded. "My child is not a bully!" he charged.

"I understand your concern," the vice principal said brusquely. "It can be hard for parents to come to terms with something like this. But bully-ing is a very serious issue and we don't tolerate it at our school. Our job is to keep all our children safe and make sure bullying doesn't happen here.

We take swift action when bullying occurs, which is what we're doing now."

"That's all fine and well, but my daughter is not a bully!" the father continued, his irritation growing. "Not letting a kid sit with you at lunch is hardly a crime. Maybe she had a good reason for not wanting to sit with Mary. Have you ever thought of that? What are you going to do—make all the kids sit together? Do you have a table that seats a hundred? This is crazy!"

The vice principal waited until the father calmed down a bit. "I'm sure you will agree with our need to do what's right when it comes to supporting the victims of bullying," she finally answered coolly.

"But what about my daughter?" the father demanded. "I resent the way you're characterizing her. She's a good kid. So what if she doesn't like everyone. That doesn't make her a bully. I'm sorry a kid got her feelings hurt but, honestly, nobody likes everyone."

"Your daughter needs to be held accountable for her behavior, and that's exactly what I'm going to do," the vice principal said, indicating with a nod that the meeting was over.

Later, when Mary's father returned home from his meeting with the vice principal, he told Mary what had happened. "The vice principal assured me she's going to take care of this, so you let us know if they give you any trouble with them. Okay?" he told Mary. "And I want you to tell your mom and me the minute you have trouble with any of those girls at school."

Mary shrugged her shoulders. "They're going to hate me now, Dad," she said sadly. "I got them in trouble."

"No you didn't, honey," Mary's father said, trying to reassure her. "They got themselves into trouble. You did nothing wrong, and you need to remember that. This is about them being bullies and mean girls, and that's wrong. They're going to get punished, so everything's going to be okay. Doesn't this make you feel better?"

"I guess so . . . ," Mary said haltingly.

The Aftermath

Mary returned to school the next day and was grudgingly included at lunch by her classmates. None of the other girls said anything explicit to her about what had happened—they were smart enough to know that such a move would get them into even more trouble—but they made it clear to Mary that she was not welcome in their circle. Mary tried to join in their conversation with little success and, after a number of attempts at being included in their crowd, Mary decided on her own to sit elsewhere at lunch.

The offending girls served their detentions, produced half-hearted essays on bullying, and wrote letters of apology to Mary. These came across to Mary and her parents as forced and mostly insincere, and Mary's father contacted the vice principal.

"I want the bullies to apologize to my daughter for what they did, and to *really mean it!*" he said.

"I'm sure they do," the vice principal replied. "But you've got to remember that they're only 12."

"I don't care!" Mary's father exclaimed. "My daughter went through hell because of them. My wife and I went through hell, for that matter, and I want to see some resolution to this!"

"Has Mary been excluded at lunch or received any more harassing e-mails?" the vice principal asked.

"Well, no," the father admitted. "But that's not the point."

"Yes, in fact," the vice principal countered, "that *is* the point. The behavior in question has ceased. Mary is no longer being bullied. You said so yourself. I recognize that being a victim of bullying is awful, but there's nothing more I can do."

"But Mary doesn't feel any better, not really," her father lamented, "And she needs to feel better. *I* need to feel better."

Getting Stuck

Anti-Bullying education programs, policies, and responses are calls to action. *Stop bullying now! Protect victims! Don't be a bystander! Be an ally!* If we act, the thinking goes, we will stop the bullying. There is logic to this reasoning, but it doesn't solve the entire problem. In Mary's case, the intervention stopped the specific behaviors, and that's good, although such interventions don't always have this intended effect. After all was said and done, Mary still felt bad and was left out by her peers; her classmates felt resentful and angry with her and the vice principal; Mary's parents couldn't let go of the pain their daughter had suffered and they continued to fear she would get bullied again; and the bullies' parents believed their children had been misunderstood. In a word, everyone was stuck.

I became interested in our approach to bullying as I repeatedly noticed how stuck everyone seemed to feel after the fact. Rarely did I encounter victims who felt soothed or safe, bullies who demonstrated self-awareness or repentance, parents of victims whose fears had subsided, or parents of bullies who felt heard and invested in helping their children solve behavioral problems. Presumably, these are the goals that guide our anti-bullying protocols. Instead, I noticed that while everyone had a different experience after the bullying incident(s), most still felt bad. Frankly, I was surprised by this realization because I have worked with superb teachers, counselors, and administrators in many schools—and parents, in general, want what's best for their children—and yet all of us, working within the parameters of the current system, seemed to feel exhausted and often defeated on the other side of a bullying case.

This led me to wonder whether something in our approach was causing this to be the case, and if so, what it was. From my vantage point, there was no one to blame for these unsatisfactory outcomes—everyone was dedicated to making things right—and yet, despite all our efforts, something was still wrong. So, I started to think about not just bullying but how our culture thinks about bullying, how it is discussed, and how our methods of dealing with bullying shape our understanding of childhood aggression. And the first thing that struck me was the language many of us use when we talk about bullying.

Bully Language

Bully. Follower. Henchman. Passive Bully. Victim. Target. Bystander. Ally. Defender. There are a lot of different terms to describe childhood relational aggression, and many of them are new. When I started working in schools over 20 years ago, there were no specific anti-bullying policies or nomenclature, and I'd never heard the terms henchmen, bystanders or allies in relation to kids and their behavior. A generation ago a precise language to describe the kinds of harassment that can happen between kids didn't exist. Sure, the term bully existed but it was used in a general way, and kids weren't "charged" with bullying.

The fact that there wasn't a vocabulary to describe what was happening between kids didn't mean all was well. Lots of bad things happened, but they were talked about differently and, to be honest, a lot of problems were swept under the rug. In a desire to no longer do this, and to keep children safe, a way of thinking about what can go wrong and how kids can hurt one another developed. Bully Language was born. (When I use the term Bully Language throughout this chapter, I am referring to the aforementioned terms that are assigned to children in bullying situations, and the terms often used to describe the dynamics between kids.)

In theory, this was a great idea. Finally there was a way to describe problems children had in their relationships with each other, and thus help them cope. This was supposed to empower everyone. In practice, Bully Language, and the resulting conceptual framework it creates and supports, falls short of achieving these goals in ways I shall explain throughout the remainder of this chapter.

Bully Language seeks to describe painful scenarios between children. It also labels the players and implies the action that has taken place. There are two main players in the bully drama, the bully and the victim, but often there are many more and, depending on their behavior, members of the supporting cast are on one side or the other of the bully scenario; there is no middle or neutral ground described by Bully Language. Bullies are necessarily bad by definition, and they are to blame. Victims, on the other hand, are blameless, and the labels ensure this dichotomy. There is no sort-of bully, or ¾ bully, or part-time bully. In the same way there is no kind-of victim, or sort-of-target. You're either a bully, or you're not; you're either a victim, or you're not. The language is clear on this point, and it goes a long way to shaping how we think about what transpires between kids when someone gets hurts.

For example, is it possible for a bully to get hurt, too, or can a victim be partly to blame for what has happened? No, not according to Bully Language. The labels don't provide room to maneuver, to imagine a shared causality, and this keeps us stuck. The principal of a school explained it to me this way:

"One day a student came to me, crying. He was really upset because another student had punched him at recess. He said the student who hit him was a bully and that it was the other kid's fault. The student had a really bloody nose, so obviously something bad happened, and it was my job to figure it out. But if I had taken just this child's word for it, and believed everything he said without question, I wouldn't be doing my job. I've got to talk to the other student, too. And I always do this when someone makes the claim they've been bullied but the language definitely influences how we think about it. I mean, who knows? Maybe the other kid's got an even bloodier nose. The problem with our language is that it eliminates one side of the story, and if I've learned anything as a Principal it's that nothing is simple and there's *always* another side to the story."

There are a number of specific problems with Bully Language, and this principal understood the first.

Problems with Bully Language

Problem 1: Only One Side to the Story

Bully Language sets up everyone to think of only one side of the story, and to assume that there is only one side that's worth attending to. Sure, we may want to hear what the bully has to say for himself, or to know from the bystanders why they didn't do more to help the victim, but thinking of children as bullies, bystanders, and victims automatically creates a mutually agreed-upon understanding of causality, guilt, and blame. It also places the bully and the bystander on the wrong side of the narrative, which is a big hole to dig oneself out of. Even if the bully's side of the story is heard, it must necessarily fit into the preconceived notions of the bully scenario; as long as roles are assigned labels, the players' actions must fit into the bullying scenario. When children are seen as bullies, there is little they can say to successfully defend their actions or to shift an onlooker's perspective.

If we return to the case of Mary we can see this played out. One of the girls accused of bullying Mary told the vice principal that Mary could be mean to her at times, and that this meanness prompted the "bully" to say mean things about Mary in return, via e-mail. Of course, every adult is familiar with the well-worn cry, "But she started it!" and yet, what if she did? Bully Language is a one-way street, which proceeds from the bad deeds of the bully to the pain of the blameless victim, and while it's never good to diminish or deny a child's pain, this is often what happens with the use of Bully Language. What if the girl who wrote nasty things to Mary was in fact responding to a series of provocations from Mary? What if Mary, perhaps without even knowing it, had injured the feelings of this other girl in the past, and that the other girls excluded her because of her behavior?

In Mary's case, we'll never know the answer because Bully Language held sway in determining how the scenario was understood and dealt with. Only one side of the story was deemed correct, and alternative versions were never investigated, not by the vice principal or Mary's parents or Mary herself. The father of one of the accused girls tried to get another perspective considered ("Maybe she had a good reason for not wanting to sit with Mary"), but to no avail, and the girl who wrote the e-mail quickly found that her side of the story was essentially meaningless in constructing the narrative that would be considered the "truth." And all of this makes sense if we are determined to rely on labels to describe what happened. It's just not possible to label kids and their behavior and expect much else.

One scenario between kids that I see played out often goes like this. One child subtly (or not so subtly) annoys another child. Generally the behavior is a way for one child to get attention from the other, or even to provoke a response. To this end I have seen kids poke other kids, say the same thing again and again, repeatedly violate personal space, scribble things on notebooks, or peer over a shoulder while another kid is working—just annoying stuff, the kinds of behaviors that are designed to irritate (and which are all perfectly normal, by the way, although certainly irritating). So, one kid annoys and provokes another child in this way until the other kid can't stand it anymore. Of course, the acceptable response is for the annoyed kid to tell the annoying kid to stop it, and maybe they do. If the behavior continues, kids take action in response. A shout, a shove, a punch, or a push—anything to get the annoying kid to just go away.

All of this sounds pretty harmless, and for the most part it is, but I have seen scenarios like this escalate to the use of Bully Language, at which point the understanding of the situation shifts dramatically.

Jonah's situation is such a case. Every day Jonah, a 5th grader, played at recess with his friends, including Danny, someone he'd known since early childhood. Jonah and Danny's mothers were good friends and the boys often played together outside of school and on weekends. But the relationship had its ups and downs, as many relationships do. For instance, Jonah often wanted to play with kids at school other than Danny and Danny didn't always feel included by the extended group. When Jonah hung out with his other friends, Danny would sometimes stand on the periphery of the group and try to engage Jonah physically. He would poke Jonah, throw small rocks at him, say things about him underneath his breath, and try to keep Jonah's attention on him. It worked, although it didn't have the effect Danny was looking for. Jonah, annoyed by Danny's behavior, went to ever-greater lengths to keep him out of the group and even went so far as to shove him on occasion when Danny hovered.

Not surprisingly, this behavior upset Danny, but it incensed his mother, who thought Jonah's behavior was unacceptable. In fact, after Danny came home from school complaining about Jonah yet again, Danny's mother cried foul. Or, more accurately, she cried *bully*. Danny's mother picked up the phone and called Jonah's mother.

"Jonah is bullying Danny!" she declared. "This has got to stop!"

"What are you talking about?" Jonah's mother replied.

"Jonah bullies Danny at recess. He keeps him out of his group and makes sure none of the other boys want to play with Danny. And now he's started to push Danny to the ground whenever Danny tries to talk to him. I'm telling you *this has got to stop!*" Danny's mother said angrily before hanging up the phone.

Jonah's mother felt she had just been blindsided. When she picked Jonah up from school that day, she asked him what was going on.

"Is it true? Did you shove Danny to the ground?" she asked.

"Yeah, I guess so, after he was bugging me and the other guys, and after he poked me for about the millionth time. I just couldn't help it, so I pushed him. He acts so weird when I hang out with my other friends at school. It's not like when it's just the two of us," Jonah explained.

"Well, I don't care how annoying he is. I don't want you to shove him again, do you understand?" Jonah's mother told him. Jonah nodded. "Fine, but he can be such a baby, Mom."

Danny's mother asked questions of her own when she picked Danny up from school that day. "What happened today, honey? Any more trouble with Jonah?"

It was clear Danny was upset. He reported that the dynamic between the two boys hadn't changed, and that he had once again found himself on the receiving end of a shove. As soon as they got home, Danny's mother called Jonah's mother again.

"It happened again!" she declared. "Jonah shoved Danny again today at recess."

"I know," Jonah's mother said, "And I'm so sorry. I spoke with Jonah right after school and I told him it can't happen again."

"Good!" Danny's mother said sounding exasperated.

"But . . . ," Jonah's mother said with some hesitation. "It seems as though this is going both ways."

"What do you mean?" Danny's mother demanded.

"Well, Jonah was wrong to shove Danny, I've told him that, but apparently Danny is poking Jonah and saying things to him to provoke him. I think Jonah is getting a little frustrated and that's why he shoved Danny."

"I don't care what Danny did to him," Danny's mother replied. "Jonah's being a bully. Danny is hurt and feeling intimidated."

"I understand that," Jonah's mother said, feeling exasperated herself. "But I think there may be two sides to the story here. Maybe it would help if Danny backed off a little bit."

"This is ridiculous! My son is being bullied every day and you think it's his fault?"

They were at an impasse, one that is not atypical once Bully Language is introduced. The term bully creates a divide in situations like this, where one person's story is right and the other's is wrong, or more accurately, irrelevant. Danny's mother didn't deny that her son behaved in certain ways, but his behavior didn't matter once Jonah became a bully. With Bully Language, the bully's behavior reaches a level that makes all other behavior pale by comparison, no matter how much that behavior contributes to the situation.

This is especially true if the behavior on the part of the apparent aggressor is egregious, which Jonah's was not. Mark, on the other hand, acted in a way that made everyone else's behavior seem tame.

Mark, an 8th grade student, rode the bus to school every day and sat with a group of classmates near the back, well beyond the view of the driver. At the beginning the school year, Antonio, another 8th grader, sat behind Mark and repeatedly made comments to him about his hair, clothes, athletic prowess—anything he could think of. At first, Mark tried to ignore him, or say something dismissive in return.

"Whatever, Antonio," he might say to another of Antonio's comments, and return to looking at his homework. But Antonio kept at it. Soon, the verbal jabs became more taunting in nature. But Mark managed to keep his cool even though he was starting to feel bad every time he got on the bus. One day, after Antonio had been bothering Mark non-stop throughout the ride, Mark couldn't take it anymore. After Antonio made a particularly offensive comment, Mark put away his books in his back pack, turned around to look at Antonio, and punched him hard in the face. "Shut up, you asshole!" Mark said.

Antonio reeled back into his seat and put his hands over his face. Blood streamed out of his nose, and the other boys shouted for the bus driver. Soon afterward, the bus was pulled to the side of the road, the principal was called, and in very short order Mark was expelled from school. The school's Zero Tolerance clause in its Anti-Bullying policy required that such displays of violence be dealt with immediately and definitively but it did not require that the other side of the story be told. Mark hit Antonio. Antonio got hurt, and that was the end of story, or at least one side of it.

I am not suggesting that Mark shouldn't have faced consequences for his actions—he should have. But when only one side of the story gets told, or when only one side gets treated as valid, it is a disservice to both children. Mark's actions as the bully could just as well have be understood as those of someone who was standing up to a bully, but this side of the story didn't get much airtime. The principal couldn't afford to be seen as being soft on violence, and so Mark had to go. And in making such a swift and definitive decision, the principal avoided delving into the complexities of the situation.

One website that likens bullies to small scale terrorists sums up this one-sided viewpoint perfectly when it declares, "The bully is the root of the problem."[1]

Problem 2: It Makes Things Easier, Not Better

Another problem with Bully Language is that it simplifies situations that are usually complex. For instance, Mark's situation wasn't simple, and yet the principal's solution to it was, and this got him and everyone else off the hook for having to think too hard about things. What if Mark really was acting in self-defense and Antonio was more of the aggressor in their relationship? This would have been a much more complicated situation to deal with. Antonio would then have had to face consequences for his behavior, although perhaps different consequences than Mark, and then Mark may not have been dealt with as harshly. But if Mark hadn't been expelled because of the mitigating circumstances of Antonio's provocative behavior, then the school's Zero Tolerance policy would have been tested. As you can see, things can get messy quickly in real situations, but Bully Language smooths them right out again.

Many Anti-Bullying education initiatives start with labels in an effort to simplify complex situations for children, and this makes sense. *Here's the bully, here's the victim, here's the bystander,* and *you should be an ally.* The message is: the bully is the bad guy, the victim is the good guy (or at least the innocent guy), and an ally can make the situation better. These labels are used to teach children concepts such as *it's wrong to hurt others, you should seek help when you feel hurt,* and *you should stick up for your friends.* Bully Language allows kids to quickly grasp and conceptualize simple truths, but it's important to recognize that the bully labels scrub away important nuances, as they did in all of the above situations. I have yet to come across a bully situation that boiled down to the simple bully-victim formula; every single situation I have dealt with has been more complicated than this but Bully Language allows and sometimes prevents those involved from diving into more complex terrain.

Why? Because labels appeal to brains that think simply, that see the world in absolute terms—to children's brains, that is, especially young

---

1.BullyPolice.com, www.bullypolice.org/grade.html

children's brains. Children can't help it that they think this way. Therefore, it is our responsibility, using our adult brains—which have the capacity for abstract thought—not to fall into the trap of ignoring the inherent complexity of most bully situations, regardless of our competing need to instruct children to make a point. Children need clarity and limits, and Bully Language helps to establish these things, but we shouldn't value our children's need to understand things over our own need to understand things in much more complex ways.

Bully and victim labels deny us the opportunity to contemplate the shades of gray, and to instruct our children to do the same. The logic that follows from our labels is:

1. There's only one explanation to a situation.

2. Blame and responsibility cannot be shared.

3. People can't play multiple roles.

4. The situation is simple, therefore

5. The solution is clear and straightforward, equitable and just.

I am all for making things simple for the sake of instruction, but not when it's at the expense of the greater truth, which often happens with bullying situations. Just ask Mark. He learned this lesson the hard way.

Problem 3: Ignore Context, Lose Compassion

Another hazard of taking the simple course charted by bully labels is that the labels don't require those who use them to consider the larger context of a situation between kids. Why worry about context when the labels tell us the whole story?

I recently spoke with a woman whose situation illustrates this point. When I told her I was writing a book on bullying, she responded, "Oh, good! Have I got a case for you!" Before I could tell her that my take on bullying was a little different than most, she launched into her story. She reported that there was a terrible problem with bullying at her daughter's school, and that a new girl was causing endless trouble in the 4th grade. Christy, 10, had recently transferred to the school. She'd had problems fitting in at her former school, and as this mother said to me, "Now I know why." Apparently, Christy was intent on being the center of a group of girls that excluded and taunted others during recess. Christy could be vicious to the people she had chosen to exclude, and clearly many of her peers were intimidated by her, even scared, which is why many either colluded with her behavior (as passive bullies) or did nothing to stop it (as bystanders).

Christy, it seems, had taken over the playground in a very short period of time, and this mother, and many other parents, had started to refer to her as "the Devil," sometimes in front of their own children. The woman expressed real hatred toward Christy. "She's a classic bully," she said dismissively.

It was clear Christy had an immediate and negative impact on her environment, and that her presence was causing real problems, not least of which was that otherwise compassionate and understanding adults had no qualms about writing her off because of her selective bad behavior (apparently Christy was better in the classroom setting than at recess). When I asked this mother if she knew anything about Christy's home life or history, she looked at me quizzically. "What does that matter? She's a bully."

"Well, it matters a lot," I said. "If this kid has adults calling her the Devil, it might help to know what her deal is."

It turns out the woman knew quite a bit about Christy's history (theirs was a small school), most notably that Christy had been adopted from an orphanage in Eastern Europe when she was about 2 years old. I nodded my head when I heard this, and maybe said "Ah, ha," or something, because the woman looked at me intently and asked, "Why is that so important?"

"Kids who are adopted later on can have some issues with attachment,"[2] I explained. "Not all of them do, of course, but it's not uncommon. Put it this way, even if Christy had a great experience in the orphanage and had lots of caring and loving adults around her—and this is the best-case scenario—imagine what it would have been like to leave them without notice. A two-year-old kid doesn't know what's happening when she gets adopted. All she knows is that one day she's in a new place, with new people around her, and, in her case, in a new country and culture."

I could see the woman taking all of this in.

---

2. My comments about Christy's particular situation are about her case only and should not be applied to adoption in general.

"And so let's say everything's been fine for Christy since then," I continued. "She might understandably still have difficulty with transitions. Let's see, she just transferred to a new school, and even if she hated her old school, change is a challenge, and she might also believe that she had to transfer because people at her old school thought she was bad. Now she's in a new group of kids, all of whom know each other, and she's the new kid on the block again. If I were her I'd be working hard not to be the one excluded, too."

"That makes sense," the woman replied. We sat in silence for a while before I made my final comment.

"And now Christy is in an environment where adults refer to her as the Devil. Kids aren't stupid. They know when people don't like them. Can you imagine how it feels for a 10-year-old to have most of her classmates' parents despise her?"

The woman gasped. "Oh, my God," she said. "I can't believe I've vilified her like this. I feel terrible!"

This is the power of context. It can shift perspective dramatically, and it usually serves to soften the edges of the fixed view created by labels. But note well that context should never be used as an excuse for bad behavior. Context provides explanations, not excuses. Understanding the context of someone like Christy's situation doesn't mean she should get away with her misbehavior. Christy and all the other misbehaving children need help from adults who really care about them, not from adults who refer to them as devils. When one is empowered by labels to see a devil/bully in a misbehaving child, then it's hard to care for that child; most people don't invest time and effort helping a cause that is so categorically lost. On the other hand, when there is a child who's in pain, and whose behavior may be an expression of something deeper, then most people can invest in helping that child learn and grow.

For Christy, it was important for adults to understand her past in order to have compassion for her, but it's also important to understand what's happening currently to get the full picture. David's case is a good example.

David, 7, arrived at school every morning, acting like a tyrant. All of the second graders were supposed to go directly to their cubby when they got to school, hang up their jackets, take out their homework folders, and put away their backpacks. Most children had no problem with this routine, but David did. When David got to his cubby, he threw his jacket and backpack on the floor and searched for the nearest classmate to bother. He would approach other children and start irritating them, sometimes by poking them or shoving them. Everyone dreaded David's arrival in the morning, especially the other parents who were present to help their own children with their morning routines. They bristled as David entered the hallway, waiting to see what his behavior would bring each day, and close behind David was his mother, who had as little control of David as David did himself.

When David threw his jacket and backpack on the floor, rather than instructing him to pick them up, or providing some structure and discipline for David, his mother simply picked up after him, leaving him free to bother other children. She didn't seem to notice how the other parents glared at her, or how they tried to keep their own children out of David's way. His mother seemed as perplexed and frustrated by David's behavior as anyone, but it was her job to do something about it, and she simply couldn't. As a single mother holding down two jobs, David's mother felt overwhelmed by life, not just by David. David could sense this, and her situation made him feel overwhelmed, too.

David's behavior at school was a reaction to something bigger than what was in front of him, as most behavior is. In this case, it was to a world that seemed unable to give him the kind of limits he needed. When the parents in the hallway called David a bully, which they did, and sometimes to his face, they were getting it wrong. David wasn't a bully as much as he was a kid who wasn't getting what he needed from the adults around him. He needed help, as did his mother, but without considering the context, other couldn't give David the help he needed. Any intervention had to be much bigger than just dealing with David's behavior in the school hallways, although this also needed attention. David needed the world to understand that he didn't exist in isolation, and that calling him a bully served to isolate him even more.

Problem 4: The Us vs. Them Mentality

One thing that struck me about both David and Christy's cases was how effectively a group of otherwise compassionate adults bonded together over their mutual dislike of a child. In Christy's case, her devilishness was often the subject of carpool conversations and parents reached out and supported each other in their shared disdain for Christy. The parents found a common ground in their negative feelings about Christy, and in joining together they made sure their own children were protected from similar scrutiny and judgment. What they experienced as a group, with Christy's behavior to galvanize them, was powerful. They had a cause. They were on a mission. It was *us versus them* (or, as in the above case, *us versus the devil*), and they believed they were right.

This also happened with David, and in David's case the parents joined together against David's mother as well, making it even harder for them to care about David. The 2nd grade parents couldn't stand David, and they had no difficulty expressing their disdain. It almost felt good to hate him, and this made a lot of sense. David's behavior *was* terrible, no question about it, and there is something extremely satisfying to the other parents about being right.

Being right feels great, and using labels, and the absolute thinking that comes with them, makes being right feel even better. With no ambiguity to get in the way, Bully Language provides an almost thrilling sense of righteousness to those on the victim's side of the divide, even if it's at the expense of a child. As soon as the middle ground of context enters the picture, such righteousness has to be reevaluated, and this takes effort. It's much easier to leave the situation unexamined than to do the work necessary to understand what's going on.

One thing I've noticed about Bully Language is how quickly it can turn potential allies into enemies. This happened with Jonah and Danny's mothers, who had been good friends until their sons started having problems with each other. Danny's mother, empowered by Bully Language, felt unabashedly right in her stance (since bullies are bad). Her sense that she was right gradually turned into self-righteousness, and soon Jonah's mother became her former friend. Unfortunately, Bully Language didn't provide Danny's mother with what she really needed, which was the option of working with Jonah's mother to help their sons. The labels pitted Danny's mother against her friend, and Jonah's mother soon had no option but to see Danny's mother from across a great divide.

I have found this *us versus them* mentality particularly difficult to bridge when trying to get a sense of the so-called victim's responsibility in the situation. Those who adhere to the use of labels can take great offense when a victim is questioned. *Blaming the victim* is something everyone wants to avoid, and as long as children who feel hurt are seen only as victims, this is logical. This point was hit home for me when I was once accused of not having compassion for a so-called victim because I sought to learn how she might have contributed to the situation.

"But she's the victim!" many around me cried. "She had nothing to do with it!" I had to tread with extreme care as I tried to unravel the details of the situation, and my hands were tied for the most part because the use of labels meant that judgment about the situation had already been rendered.

Problem 5: The Presumption of Guilt

Most children have been taught to report bullying immediately. Once a report is made, most schools with Anti-Bullying policies have to immediately initiate a carefully crafted protocol, even if the charges don't seem that serious. In my experience, once the term bully is used, schools have no choice but to respond, both in order to keep kids safe and, to be honest, to cover their rears. If they rely on their own judgment instead of a scripted procedure they could not only get sued, but parents could go onto the Internet and start posting about the school's problem with bullying, and its lack of responsiveness to it. The threat of having a school charged with being soft on bullying has many people running scared, so they willingly follow procedures even in situations when they know there are more effective ways to proceed.

I don't fault schools for having strict policies about keeping kids safe. The problem arises when the methods of response don't allow for due process or a presumption of innocence. When bullying is reported—even if the case doesn't have merit—bully labels are generally employed, which means the accused is seen as a bully and the accuser is seen as a victim, long before actual responsibility can be fairly determined. This is most troubling when adults are the ones making the initial charge, as Danny's mother was. How does a child, with the reasoning power of a young brain, stand up to that?

This is what happened in a case early in my career. A middle school girl complained to some teachers that a group of classmates was teasing her and calling her names. The teachers, knowing that the accused clique of girls had a lot of social power, encouraged the girl who was feeling hurt to inform them whenever she felt excluded or picked on. She did as she was told, and it wasn't long before the teachers started to refer to the clique of girls as bullies. One teacher even suggested that the accused girls be expelled from school and criminally charged with harassment, all before a thorough investigation had been conducted or any of the girls had been questioned. The presumption in this case, as in many I have dealt with, was "guilty until proven innocent," and Bully Language allows us to get away with this.

This was the case that taught me how damning and blinding Bully Language can be. Under the guise of standing up for the victim, otherwise reasonable adults were prepared to kick kids out of school without any crime being witnessed, testimony heard, or context considered. The authority to do this came solely from using the terms bully and victim. It didn't cross anyone's mind to consider how the other 13-year-olds in this case were being treated, or that they were being excoriated by adults who were being paid to consider their welfare too. To repeat, the girls in question were 13 years old, and they were being torn apart by adults—*adults*—who wielded the power to accuse, try, and condemn them without giving a second thought to their rights. To the adults in this situation, the bullies didn't have rights because they were bullies.

Problem 6: The String of Pearls Effect

Another problem with Bully Language is something I call the String of Pearls Effect. When a child is labeled a bully, this has the effect of coloring everyone's view of that child's past and future behavior.

"I'm not surprised," adults say of a misbehaving child who's gotten into trouble as a bully. "He's been like this since he was little—once a bully, always a bully, I suppose."

Linking past behavior with present circumstances in this manner serves to justify the use of the label, which then adds credence to the idea that the problem has always been brewing, and that it will always be there. Once the past has served to bolster the impressions of the present, the obvious next step is to project into the future and start looking for evidence of bullying behavior in everything the child does going forward. What is to stop us from doing this? Certainly not how we talk about the situation, which serves to connect the child's past and future like a string of pearls. This leaves the child damned if he does and damned if he doesn't, and with much more to atone for than his present misdeeds.

The String of Pearls Effect unwittingly leaves us with the impression that children, or at least children labeled as bullies, don't change, and this is tragic. Childhood is all about change and children, even misbehaving children, make huge strides in their learning and behavior all the time, sometimes daily. To saddle them, and us, with the idea that they don't change by creating the String of Pearls Effect doesn't help anyone, as Janet's case demonstrates.

Janet was a bright, engaged, and popular 9th grader. She was a leader among her peers, but sometimes she was followed for all the wrong reasons. Janet could be mean, catty, exclusive, cruel, and she was feared more than liked by her classmates (and by some of her teachers).

At the end of every school year, the teachers at Janet's school got together to discuss the students who were moving up to the next grade, as a way to prep the new teachers about what to expect. When it came time to discuss the rising 10th graders, Janet's name was at the top of the list. "You better watch out," Janet's current math teacher told his colleagues. "She's the Queen Bee of the Mean Girls. She can be awful."

"Yeah," another chimed in. "Janet's posse is a force to contend with. We call them the tornadoes because they destroy everything in their path."

The 10th grade teachers heard this and gave each other wary looks. All of them made mental notes to watch out for Janet and her gang. Not surprisingly, when the school year started, all of Janet's teachers had already formed an impression of her, and it wasn't a good one. They paid attention to her every move and read something negative into almost all of them. If Janet was seen talking to a friend, she was gossiping. If she chose to sit beside one person and not another, she was excluding someone. If she rolled her eyes or flipped her hair, she was orchestrating something. Janet's behavior was scrutinized in a way no other student's was, and whatever she was doing her teachers assumed it was bad.

Labeling Janet a Mean Girl clouded her teachers' view of everything she did, including her work as a student. How could a Mean Girl be serious about her studies, they wondered? How could she be a really good student? When any trouble arose in the classroom, Janet was the first suspect, all because her teachers had been set up to assume the worst about her. This is the String of Pearls Effect in action. As with every other form of prejudice, Janet had to work twice as hard as her peers to earn her teachers' respect and make them believe she was the same as every other teenager: prone to making mistakes.

The String of Pearls Effect takes incidents from a child's life and strings them together such that they make a coherent whole; it creates a narrative. When we consider incidents of misbehavior as discrete events, we deal with them in the moment. When we see them as connected, we create a story about a child that can hang around her neck like an albatross. In this way, events take on much more weight and import than they might otherwise—they come to *define* a child's character rather than simply *describe* her behavior.

Some would argue that this is a vital exercise; that the act of taking separate incidents and considering them together reveals a greater truth that can't be discerned in any other way. But when we do this to the degree that we damn a child, or prejudge him in a negative way, we have effectively shut ourselves off from seeing a different future for that child. And the question that remains is, *when does a bully stop being a bully?*

When children are labeled bullies, and when past behaviors are automatically connected to present and future behavior, a powerful momentum is created. Where does this process end? When a child's behavior changes? For how long must the child be reformed before the label is dropped and his record is expunged? Does he stop being a bully when we forgive him and change our opinion? Or maybe the label is withdrawn when he advances to the next grade (although this didn't happen in Janet's case), graduates, or moves to another town—that is, when no one is left to remember the past.

Bully Language sets children up for long sentences. Once a child is labeled, it is much harder for those around him to let go. "He used to be such a bully," is one way to refer to a reformed child, although the label still allows for a constant reminder of past sins and an urging for caution in the present and future. "Who would have guessed he'd come this far?" is another backhanded compliment. But the label continues to cast a long shadow, as these statements attest.

If Janet's teachers had referred to her as stupid (which they wouldn't have in this day and age, fortunately), they would have blinded themselves to her capacity for learning and growth. As a stupid student, Janet's good grade on a test would have been seen as an aberration, and a well-written paper as proof that she got help from someone else. We try hard not to damn children in this regard and yet we continue to do so with impunity when it comes to their bad behavior. In Janet's case, it took an open-minded English teacher to slowly change people's view of her.

As this teacher read Janet's class journal, she saw a side of Janet that others didn't—or couldn't—see because they had already written her off. What she saw was not a perfect person, or one who didn't struggle with her behavior, but one who had many good attributes in addition to her challenging ones. She saw Janet's pain and insecurity and capacity for self-reflection, qualities which made her much more sympathetic. With this insight, Janet's teacher was able to stop seeing Janet's behavior as an inevitable string of pearls, and she stopped writing her off as a result.

Problem 7: When You Use Labels, You Lose Parents

Bully Language writes off more than just the bullies; it also writes off the parents of the kids being labeled as bullies, and that's another shame. When children are labeled as bullies, the very people who are most invested in their growth and development—their parents—become alienated. If you still need convincing that bully labels are harmful, imagine that your child (or a child you care for) has been called a bully. How would that make you feel? If you're like most parents, it would make you feel all kinds of things, none of them positive: defensive, angry, possibly scared. It certainly wouldn't make you feel like you wanted to ally with the person labeling your child, even if you knew your child had done something wrong.

Take Ann, for example. Ann's daughter Isabelle, 15, went to school with Heather. The two girls had been good friends during elementary school but now, as freshmen, they were growing apart. Isabelle wanted to hang out with a different crowd and, like many kids in high school, she set about reinventing herself by cutting ties with her past. While she was unsure of herself in many ways, Isabelle was certain she didn't want to be close friends with Heather anymore. "Friends Light" was how Isabelle described their new relationship.

This was Isabelle's side of the story. From Heather's perspective, on the other hand, Isabelle wasn't just hanging out with a new crowd, she was waging a veritable war against her. Heather was distraught by things Isabelle posted on her Facebook page—hurtful and personal things about Heather—and by referring to social events that Heather wasn't invited to. Heather believed Isabelle got other girls to join in, and that Isabelle was actively trying to humiliate and torment her. It got to the point where Heather felt she couldn't log onto Facebook without reading something disparaging about herself, courtesy of Isabelle.

After weeks of listening to her daughter cry, complain of stomach aches, and beg to be allowed to stay home from school, Heather's mother, Barbara, had enough. She resolved to call Ann, whom she'd known since their daughters were young, and confront her about Isabelle's behavior. "We both knew this was going to happen one day," Barbara said, dispensing with the pleasantries she usually offered at the start of a conversation. "There's a bully in every crowd, and your daughter is it."

Ann didn't know what to make of the accusation. She knew Isabelle and Heather weren't good friends anymore, but she didn't know things had gotten this bad.

She was upset to hear someone cast her daughter in such a negative light, but she wanted to know more about what was happening between the girls.

"Maybe there's an explanation," Ann began.

"I don't want to hear any excuses!" Barbara seethed, cutting Ann off. "Not from you or Isabelle. Heather is getting cyber-bullied almost every day, and Isabelle is behind it!"

As Ann listened to Barbara's accusations, she became increasingly uncomfortable. She sensed Barbara's distress, but her rage was also unmistakable, and Ann couldn't help but feel protective of her child. As Barbara continued her rant against Isabelle, Ann became less and less inclined to believe anything she said. When Barbara wouldn't let her get a word in edgewise, Ann finally said, "Please don't ever speak to me this way again," and hung up the phone.

In my experience, parents whose children are labeled bullies don't need to be confronted with the kind of anger that Barbara directed towards Ann to get turned off. Even the most pleasant tone doesn't soften the blow of the bully label. The label suggests that the person using it is not invested in helping the accused child. Often people using the label come across as being more interested in discharging their own anger and frustration than in anything else, although they may not realize it. In their desire to protect children, and in their fear that a child's pain may continue, they come from a very reactive place, and this is completely understandable. The problem is, it usually backfires, as it did with Ann.

If Barbara's goal was to get Isabelle to stop doing what she was doing, calling her a bully wasn't an effective strategy. Devising helpful strategies isn't the rationale behind Bully Language. Instead, using Bully Language is more about assigning blame and creating the illusion of simple solutions than anything else, something the parents of accused children understand intuitively. To this end, Ann was *less* inclined after the phone call to see things from Barbara's perspective, and *more* inclined to consider that whatever Isabelle was doing to Heather might be justified.

It's one thing for parents to have other parents accuse their children of bullying, as in Ann's case. It's quite another to hear it from a school. If she'd wanted, Ann could have completely disregarded what Barbara said, and she could have chalked it up to hysteria on Barbara's part. But when a school accuses a child of bullying, parents must respond, and this brings the problem of using the bully label to a whole new level. This was Frank's situation.

One day, Frank got a call from the principal of his son's elementary school. She asked Frank to come in immediately because Frank's son, Aidan, 6, had been bullying other children, apparently for weeks. Frank rushed to the school and was met by not only the principal, but also by Aidan's teacher and the school counselor. The group took their seats and began the discussion by listing the numerous occasions that Aidan bullied his classmates. Apparently, Aidan had trouble settling down in the classroom and often lashed out at others. Then he had difficulty with transitions and caused trouble whenever the group needed to move on to its next activity. And recess was just a nightmare for everyone, according to the group, as Aidan ran roughshod over his mostly smaller classmates. Frank listened to all of this, feeling stunned and ashamed.

"I had no idea," he said.

"Well, we don't tolerate bullying at our school, so Aidan's behavior has to change fast," the principal said decisively. "Does Aidan bully outside of school?" she asked.

Frank was still trying to wrap his mind around all of the accusations. He wasn't ready to accept that his child was a bully.

"No," Frank finally said. "Aidan is pretty good at home. He's very energetic, that's for sure, but he gets along with some of the neighborhood kids pretty well. And he's close with his older brother."

The rest of the group eyed each other as Frank reported this, then the school counselor responded. "Perhaps Aidan is getting bullied at home by your older son," she said. "This may explain why he's bullying all of his classmates at school."

This was more than Frank could handle. "Excuse me?" he said.

"Often bullies have been bullied themselves, and that's why they behave the way they do. Your son probably learned how to bully from someone close to him, maybe your other son," the school counselor said. Frank was silent. After a moment, the counselor added, "Or maybe his bullying comes from his interactions with other family members."

This was *way* more than Frank could handle. He was willing to entertain the idea that Aidan was having problems at school—Frank himself had had some trouble of his own as a kid—but he wasn't willing to sit back passively while his entire family was maligned in this way, without real discussion of Aidan's welfare.

"I resent this," Frank shot back. "There's nothing wrong with my family. Aidan is a normal kid. And my other son is normal, too," he said defensively.

By this point, it's fair to say that the school had lost Frank as an ally, and this is really tragic. Frank, in fact, had done everything right—he behaved the way responsive parents should behave, and in the way schools hope parents will behave when there's a problem. He'd come to the school immediately upon request and was open to hearing what the group had to say about his son. He wasn't closed off to the idea that Aidan needed help, and he was ready to work with the team to figure out a solution.

Unfortunately, nothing the group said to Frank suggested that its goal was to provide help for him or his family. Rather, they remained focused on the problem (as they viewed it), and their repeated use of labels underscored this for Frank. Frank needed to hear about possible solutions to the problem, and suggestions about what he could do to help. *What did the group propose he do with Aidan*, he wondered, and *what would improvement look like?* These were the things Frank needed to hear, but the group's insistence that Frank see his son, and possibly both of his sons, as bullies got them nowhere. Instead, this tactic made Frank angry and resistant, and it gave the group the fuel it needed to believe that the problem, and the solution, lay solely with Frank's family.

This is what Bully Language does inadvertently—it targets, describes, and perpetuates a problem rather than focuses on a solution. In Frank's case, it created an enormous hurdle to going forward, and in fact it set things back immeasurably. Frank left the meeting questioning whether his son was at the right school, not thinking about how he could help his son with his behavior. If the school had avoided using bully labels, especially with a willing and open parent such as Frank, the results would have been markedly different, and the group could have worked together to support Aidan overcome his challenges.

Sometimes people use Bully Language for the express purpose of creating the kind of divide Frank experienced at Aidan's school. When schools wish to get rid of a student, or when they want to express anger without being direct, they have Bully Language as a tool to meet these goals. But even in these cases, Bully Language is not the most effective way to proceed. If Aidan's teachers actually believed that he needed a different learning environment, inciting Frank's ire didn't really help, and it certainly didn't do anything for Aidan. Bully Language doesn't help children who need it the most.

Problem 8: It Makes Children the Enemy

Bully Language also allows its users to distance themselves from the fact that when they talk about bullies and victims and bystanders and allies, they are talking about *children:* little people whose brains are not yet fully developed (more on this in Chapter 3), who haven't yet learned all the lessons they need to learn (and that we need to teach them), and who make mistakes—kids. Bully Language empowers its users to write off children, to see them as beyond redemption, and to feel good in the process. I don't see the adults who use Bully Language scrutinizing or judging their own behavior to any great degree, but when it comes to kids misbehaving, watch out. The kids who are labeled as bullies are demonized without a second thought, and the adults who do it think they are doing the right thing.

Most anti-bullying education initiatives are predicated on the idea that attaching labels to the action and players involved in childhood misbehavior is an essential part of stopping that behavior. This presumption gives adults (and children) license to apply bully labels very liberally— this is what they've been told to do—which in essence gives everyone permission to see selected children as being beyond hope. But there's something bigger going on here. Our culture is looking for someone to blame and right now it's the bully. I doubt most adults believe children are the source of all our problems (okay, maybe they think teenagers are, but this happens in every generation), but bullies? Now that's a different story: *bullies—there's a problem*. When it comes to bullies, they must be resisted, punished, and legislated against. And who is this *them* we're talking about again? Kids.

I have dealt with adults who used terms such as abusive, terrorizing, tormenting, and hateful to describe children. I have no doubt that the children in question—and all children, for that matter—behave in ways that are pretty bad at times. But Bully Language has given its users permission to take absolute positions against children and to stain their characters as a result, and to do so, at times, without much cause, or without the requirement for any self-reflection. To call a seven-year-old child an abusive bully is to have no real idea of what abuse is all about, or what seven-year-olds are all about. But it's a good way to get people's attention and to deflect any responsibility for a difficult situation away from oneself and onto a child. *A child.*

Notice how the terms we use evoke different responses in our minds. Consider, for example, the terms *child* versus *bully*. A child is innocent and playful and lovable and maybe misguided at times—and maybe a child drives us crazy and we can't wait for her to grow up and get out of the house—but we want to protect her, nurture her, and we seek to understand her. A bully, on the other hand, is by definition guilty and hateful and out of control, and we actively vilify and seek to punish her. And make no mistake: we can be talking about the same child when we use these terms. Language really does matter; it's not just an issue of semantics.

Let me offer an example.

There was an article in my local newspaper (the online edition) about an incident between two boys coming off a school bus. The headline read *Judge Frees Teen Who Stabbed School Bully to Death*. The boys in question were 14 and 16 years old. The boys got off the bus separately but crossed paths soon afterwards. An altercation occurred and, according to the article, the younger boy stabbed the older boy to death. The older boy was not armed and was stabbed 12 times. The article described the older boy as a bully, and reported that he had harassed the younger boy earlier on the bus.

These were the "facts" provided in the article: two boys, one unarmed and a bully, the other one armed and a victim; an altercation occurred; one boy stabbed the other resulting in death. There was nothing specific in the article about what had happened on the bus, just the "fact" that the older boy, the one who was killed, was characterized as a bully. Also, there was nothing in this specific article about the "bully" pursuing the other boy off the bus or provoking him in any way. (I say this to emphasize simply what the article reported, not what necessarily happened, that the boy who was killed was not identified by his specific behavior, he was just labeled as a bully.)

At the end of the article, readers were invited to post responses.[3] Based on nothing more than the fact that the boy who was killed had been characterized and labeled as a bully, readers posted comments such as:

- I bet there won't be anymore bullying this kid has to put [up] with. Kudos to him.

- Justice is served!!

- Bully learned this lesson the hard way.

- Death is a severe penalty to pay for being a bully, but that is

---

3 From SFGate.com (San Francisco Chronicle), January 5, 2012.

the risk that bullies take. Bully the wrong guy and you end up stabbed and bleeding to death in the street. Justice was served.

- Too bad he was a bully, but . . . kudos to the kid who defended himself, and . . . good riddance to the bully!
- Finally, a story with a happy ending :-)
- Although I do not condone stabbing a bully to death, the bully got what was coming to him. Sadly, it's the bully's parents who are responsible for raising him to bully other kids. Still, he won't be bullying any more kids and that is a good thing.
- You know—just fork bullies—they make life hell just for their own enjoyment—they deserve to die.

They deserve to die. A 16-year-old child deserves to die, and kudos to the kid that killed him. Please note once again that the article didn't specify what this child, the "bully," had done (and I'm sure he did something, but the point is that the article didn't spell it out). But based on nothing, absolutely nothing, other than characterizing the kid as a bully, these readers felt empowered to herald and justify the death/murder of a child. *A child.*

This is what Bully Language does. It gives adults (and I assume the above comments were posted by adults) license to talk this way about children, and to feel justified in doing so. In this case, it granted permission to newspaper readers to feel righteous in celebrating the murder of a child—a child whose behavior was not spelled out, whose sins were not enumerated, but who, according to the readers/commentators—by virtue of the fact of being labeled a bully—deserved to die. They should be ashamed of themselves. But Bully Language reassures us that shame is for the bully only, not for those who use labels, and so those of us who wish to do so can cheer the vigilante from the sidelines without guilt (*just fork bullies!*), without pause, and without fear of having to look at our own reflections in the mirror.

Presumably people who commented on this article would not be so bold as to call for the forking of other children, and yet as soon as a child is called a bully, all bets are off. As this case illustrates, Bully Language invites everyone, especially those who are not directly involved, to feel satisfied that they know everything about the labeled child and the situation at hand. Certainly in this case, at least according to the comments, none of those celebrating the child's death seemed interested in learning more about the case before rendering judgment. The label was all the proof they needed.

As this case also makes clear, the Bully Language allows—or worse, encourages—those who use it to serve as witness, judge and jury, and to presume they know enough about the child in question—his entire history, the context from which he comes, all of his past "crimes," and, most importantly, his motives (for doing what, though, we're not exactly clear, because the article doesn't state any of the facts about his actions)—to celebrate his death. *Good riddance to the bully*. Would we ever say *good riddance* on the occasion of another child's death? It would be considered obscene—beyond socially unacceptable. Yet, in this case—and without even knowing anything about the case—adults lined up to spit on the grave of the bully—a child, whom they didn't know, and whose crimes were not specified. All they knew was that he was called *bully*. The kid might as well have been called Hitler; the response couldn't have been much worse.

In Chapter 2, I will explore the definition of bullying and discuss how it has expanded over the years. These days bullying covers a host of misdeeds, including name calling, teasing, and social exclusion. Perhaps the kid who was killed called the other kid names—something upsetting or hurtful, perhaps—something bad. Does he deserve to die for this? We don't know what he did, but that simply doesn't matter. He's a bully. Now he's dead. Good riddance. *They deserve to die*.

This is what Bully Language does.

Problem 9: It Pits Children Against Each Other

How can we reasonably expect children to get along with one another after they've been labeled, or after they've labeled one another, when some people think the labeled children deserve to die? If children accept or, worse yet, internalize the bully labels, they may create in their minds barriers that are impossible to scale, even in the face of lots of motivation. If you're a bully, why try to make amends when you have been written off and sentenced to death? If you're a victim, why struggle with self-reflection when you've been given license to kill (literally)? If the first goal of anti-bullying initiatives is to keep kids safe, then surely the second goal must be to help them co-exist in some fashion. Bully Language ensures that this will be an improbable, if not impossible, proposition. It's hard enough for adults to live peacefully with their enemies; how can we reasonably expect children to do so? Once children have been labeled as bullies, they truly are the enemy as long as they are seen through this prism.

Bully Language should be avoided if for no other reason than that children have to function at very close quarters with each other all day long. Once we leave school and enter the adult world, we have a lot of freedom to choose with whom we spend our days. This isn't the case for children. For kids, school is required and, in essence, it is their life. Having to go to school with people who have been labeled *bully* makes the prospect of a functional, if not happy, coexistence that much harder. Imagine if adults had to work everyday alongside people who had been labeled the enemy, enemies who had the potential to do great harm. Such a situation would not be a neutral one, by any means. Plenty of us work with people we don't like, but things would seem a lot worse if those people we didn't like or with whom we didn't get along were labeled in negative and absolute terms, such as bully.

How we think and talk about a person we don't like and whom we believe has done us harm is not a trivial matter, especially not in the mind of a child. How we choose to label a situation determines how we deal with it, and how we resolve it (or not) and move on. For example, let's say someone is causing us emotional distress. To say we don't like that person is to state our personal opinion. To say that that person has hurt us is to state our emotional reaction to an interaction or event. To say, on the other hand, that that person is a bully is to cast their character in stone, and this is a qualitatively different approach to a negative situation.

In the first two instances, we are in charge of the situation because ultimately—no matter how bad we feel—we have control over our own preference, feelings, and opinions; we can change them if we choose to do so, and we often do. In the third instance, we have absolutely no control over the situation because we have no control over someone else's character. This distinction is critical when it comes to helping children deal with the difficulties they have in their relationships with their peers. Feelings and opinions change, and sometimes quite quickly (if we give ourselves permission to change, grow, and move on). On the other hand, characterizations that arise from the use of labels do not change quickly, in part because we generally think of character as entrenched.

Samantha's case illustrates the differences between these two vantage points well.

Samantha was a 15-year-old sophomore I worked with at the beginning of my career, long before we started using Bully Language in earnest. Sam was a very attractive and likable girl but, like most of her peers, she was insecure about how she looked; she also considered herself to be overweight. She was a good student, had friends, and functioned quite well, but she really struggled when it came to her body image and her eating. By the time I started working with her, Sam had already been dieting on and off for a few years and her eating habits had crept beyond the range of healthy and normal: she cycled in and out of restrictive and binge eating and her weight fluctuated significantly as a result. Her relationship with food was very problematic, to say the least, and she was extremely self-conscious when she ate. It is fair to say that Sam was obsessed with food, eating, how she looked, and losing weight.

Sam went to a boarding school and, as a result, she had to eat all of her meals in the cafeteria—there was no place to hide—and this heightened her feelings of self-consciousness and shame. During one period when Sam was feeling particularly bad about herself, a classmate of hers, a boy named Connor, made her life even worse. When Sam would stand in the cafeteria line, Connor would come up behind her and say to the cafeteria staff, "Don't feed her—she's too fat to eat! She's a foodaholic!" He would make sure everyone in line heard him and then he would exit the cafeteria line, laughing and snickering. As Sam recalled, some of the other people in line snickered too. Not surprisingly, Sam felt humiliated. She wanted to disappear. It was bad enough that she felt terrible about her body; now Connor made sure everyone else was focused on her body too.

Sam suffered Connor's cutting and very public taunts for months. It got to the point where she would have done anything to avoid Connor, but she was required to be present at meals, plus she had to eat. In fact, eating was one of the few things that soothed her, so the more Connor teased her about her weight, the more Sam needed to eat in order to feel better about herself, and the more weight she gained as a result. It was a painful cycle that Sam couldn't seem to break, and Connor's unrelenting attention ensured that she felt pretty miserable about her life.

In today's world, Connor's treatment of Sam would no doubt be considered bullying. He verbally harassed her, repeatedly, and she felt devastated as a result. But back then, when there were no anti-bullying policies in place, Sam and I, in our work together, were left to focus on her reactions to the situation, not on intervening with or disciplining Connor. This meant we spent a lot of time discussing ways she could stand up to Connor or simply avoid him, and, most importantly, devising strategies for how she could feel better about herself. Sam spent a lot of time talking about her feelings, and in particular how much she hated Connor. *I hate that guy*, she declared on many occasions, *and I don't usually hate people*. In the absence of anti-bullying policies, hating Connor was about as far as Sam could go. She couldn't charge him with anything or label him a bully—there was no real action anyone else would take on her behalf. She couldn't get him in trouble with the school (which she didn't want to do anyway: she just wanted him to vanish), so she just dealt with her feelings, which turned out to be an advantage in the long run.

Connor's behavior and Sam's hatred of him continued unabated for more than a year. Then something happened, something truly horrible from Sam's perspective. Connor started dating one of Sam's best friends, and Sam was terrified. "That guy is poison!" Sam pleaded to her friend when she heard the news. "Can't you find anyone better than Connor? *Anyone?*" But her friend really liked Connor, and so Sam had to deal with it. By deal with it, I mean Sam had to occasionally listen to her friend say nice things about Connor. And, much to Sam's dismay, her friend's relationship with Connor lasted well beyond the average high school romance; in fact, it continued well into their senior year.

Sam's friend's relationship with Connor didn't cause Sam to like Connor all of a sudden, but it did cause her to realize that he must have another side to him. This was a good thing for her, not because Connor deserved to be liked but because Sam deserved to feel better, and the more she could see Connor in a different light, the better she felt about herself. If the community had branded Connor a bully, it would have given Sam permission in her own mind, and in the minds of others, to continue hating him, and this would have made her situation even more problematic for a number of reasons.

First, if Connor were a bully, then Sam would be a victim, and once we see ourselves as victims we have even more difficulty than usual moving on from our painful circumstances. Helping Sam deal with her feelings of self-hatred and pain was one thing, and admittedly this wasn't an easy or quick process; helping her pull herself out of being a victim would have been an altogether different prospect, and it would have taken much longer and been much more difficult.

Again, feelings change, and children know this instinctively. But labels, even to older children like Sam and Connor, are about who we are, not about what we experience, and they are very hard to shake. If Sam had seen herself as a victim, then she would have interpreted all of her negative feelings through this lens. When you're a victim, a simple bad day becomes proof that the world is against you, or that you can't do anything right. This adds a degree of importance to painful feelings, and it makes them much harder to deal with. Victims become wary of the world, and they become cynical because their experience is that it's hard to change the world around them. It's actually quite easy to change a feeling state once you know how to do it, and once your feelings change, so does the world around you; but once you're a victim, what's the point of changing your feelings? You've got a target on your back, so why bother?

The second reason it would have been bad for Sam to be a victim and for Connor to be a bully is because it would have encouraged Sam to hold onto her painful feelings long after they had served their purpose. Let me explain. Feelings are important indications of what's happening to us; they are feedback, in the same way that other bodily sensations are feedback. We have a stomachache; maybe we ate too much or someone punched us in the gut. We have a headache; maybe we're stressed out. We feel humiliated; maybe someone like Connor said something nasty.

The feedback we get, in the form of bodily sensations and feelings, alerts us to a problem. Our job is then to solve the problem. If Samantha's problem is that she feels rotten because of what Connor has said about her, then that's a problem she can solve—she can find ways to shift her rotten feeling state. But if Samantha's problem is that Connor is a bully, that's a much harder problem to solve. In fact, even the best anti-bully policy can't change Connor's character if he doesn't want to change. And if Samantha's problem is that she's a victim, that's an equally hard problem to solve, because Sam will feel like a victim as long as Connor is labeled a bully.

When kids believe they are victims, they also believe that their bad feelings are justified—that they have a right to hold onto them long after the events that caused them have passed. Have you ever heard someone in a fit of anger say, *but I have a right to feel this way?* And we do, we have the right to feel however we want, but the Buddha teaches you won't be punished for your anger, you'll be punished *by* your anger, and this is a profound truth we should teach our children. Everyone knows that negative feelings don't feel good, but when we feel justified in our negativity, it can make it much harder to process and move on. If Sam had been called a victim to Connor's bully, she would have felt justified in hating him forever, and this could have had a profound and very negative impact on her. Whereas it would sound ridiculous to say *I have a right to have headache for as long as I want*, we think it's fine to hang on to unproductive and negative feelings, and being a victim confers this right upon us.

Sam was able to get through her ordeal with Connor without the burden of labels. She got to deal with the circumstances and her feelings without having to see herself or Connor in absolute terms; they didn't get pitted against each other, like kids today do. This gave her permission in the long run to accept that Connor possessed some good qualities (despite the fact that he rarely showed them to her) and that he wasn't all bad. It also allowed her to explore why she had been vulnerable to Connor's attacks.

I ran into Sam years after she graduated, and she mentioned that Connor was one of the people she kept in touch with. *Connor?* I asked, trying to mask my surprise. Sam explained that over the years they had kept in touch through mutual friends, and that she was glad. She said that now she saw Connor as a regular guy, someone who said some mean things to her but who, it turned out, had been just as miserable in high school as she was. Sam said this had been very healing. This might not have happened if they had been labeled. Most likely, Connor would have remained a bully in Sam's eyes, and she would have had no incentive to see another side of him. It is essential to understand that seeing a different side of Connor didn't help Connor, it helped Sam, and that's the point.

Once bully labels are introduced, the negative exchanges between children become the defining moments of their relationship with one another, and they trump everything else that happens, even if it's good. Sam was lucky that she didn't have to deal with this legacy. She was open to future exchanges with Connor because he didn't live as a bully in her mind, and because she hadn't been his victim.

Problem 10: It Creates a Fixed Mindset

The final, and perhaps the most troubling, aspect of Bully Language is that it creates what Carol Dweck, a psychologist and professor at Stanford, calls a *fixed mindset*. In her bestselling book *Mindset: The New Psychology of Success*, Dweck explains that our mindset influences how we learn, tackle challenges, and think about ourselves. A mindset is nothing more than the set of beliefs we hold about things such as intelligence and personality, and yet it influences almost every aspect of our lives.

According to Dweck, there are two types of mindsets—fixed and growth. Fixed mindsets are characterized by either-or thinking, and the concept of permanence, or fixity. Those with fixed mindsets believe that traits such as intelligence and personality are carved in stone, and that failure is an identity as opposed to an action. People with growth mindsets, on the other hand, believe that traits can be developed, and that potential is something to be cultivated. Those with growth mindsets believe in development and change, and that failure is an action, not an identity.

Let's consider for a moment the implications of mindset on children and their approach to learning. When kids have a fixed mindset, for example, they believe intelligence is something that is static; that it doesn't change. The fixed mindset sounds something like this: *I am smart, which means I must always do well; if I don't do well, then maybe I'm not as smart as everyone thinks I am. I better not make any mistakes.*

When kids have a growth mindset, on the other hand, they understand that they can continue to improve if they work hard and dedicate themselves to a challenge. The growth mindset sounds something like this: *I can learn and do better if I put my mind to it, and I like the experi-ence of learning new things. If I don't do well, I know I can study harder and do better next time.* In a nutshell, a fixed mindset serves to limit achieve-ment and development while a growth mindset fosters them.

Our mindset also affects how we experience relationships, especially conflict with others. For instance, when it comes to conflict, a fixed mind-set might sound like this: *I had a fight with my friend. She's mad at me. I must have done something wrong, or maybe I am not worth being friends with. Maybe our friendship isn't worth it.* With a fixed mindset, we take things personally and tend to have an all-or-nothing reaction. In the above example, it is the self that's the problem, but it could just as easily be the other person, as in *I had a fight with my friend. She's always getting into fights. She's a bad person. I don't like her anymore.* The fixed mindset is quick to attack character as the problem, not circumstance, which means people with fixed mindsets tend to feel greater discomfort with conflict and less hope about conflict resolution.

The growth mindset has a very different response to conflict. It goes something like this: *I had a fight with a friend. I guess I'm (or she's) having a bad day. I don't like it when I have fights. I'll try to talk to her later after things cool off.* As you can see, the growth mindset separates the person from the circumstance and doesn't jump to the conclusion that all is lost. There is something inherently hopeful about the growth mindset because it rests on the assumption that change and growth are part of the equa-tion in learning and relationships, and that mistakes aren't a reflection of intelligence or character.

Dweck's work explains, in part, why some kids tend to do well in school and in relationships and others do not. Going through life tak-ing things personally, fearing failure, and believing outside circumstances can destroy your self-worth is a hard row to hoe, and those with fixed mindsets live this hardship every day. Simply put, having a fixed mindset makes life harder across the board, but it doesn't have to be. The good news is that mindsets are acquired, not hardwired, so we can adopt growth mindsets about any aspect of our lives: intelligence, personality, relation-ships, anything—and we can shape the kinds of mindset our children will have, too. How we frame things for kids will determine to a large degree what kind of mindset they develop, and therefore whether they face the world feeling confident and capable (growth mindset) or tentative and risk-averse (fixed mindset).

Dweck explains how mindsets develop. One of her most interesting findings is that praising children, particularly for their intelligence, contributes to the development of a fragile self-concept and a fixed, not growth, mindset. This might seem counterintuitive given our cultural obsession with affirmation and self-esteem, but Dweck claims that words of seeming encouragement, such as *you're so smart—you always do well* can actually undermine a child's intellectual development. Such phrases send the message that if a child is "smart," then every action or outcome from that child should appear "smart." The label *smart* thus has the effect of making children believe there is only one acceptable outcome to any effort, and that if they do not produce the intended *smart* effect, they are failures.

No one uses the term stupid anymore (at least not in the educational world), but who knew that using the term *smart* could be just as damaging? Well, it can be. Dweck's work points to the fact that it isn't whether we use positive labels instead of negative ones that's the issue, it's the fact that we're using labels at all that's the problem. So, if a positive term such as *smart* can have a negative effect on a child, just imagine what the terms *bully* and *victim* can do. These labels promote a fixed view of a given situation, and the players therein, and suggest to children that their actions are inseparable from their characters.

This also pertains to labels such as *good*. I learned this the hard way after telling a student how good she was on a number of occasions. Apparently, and without realizing it, I referred to her as *good* one too many times, and she finally called me on it.

"You know," she said. "I'm not always as good as you think I am."

Not knowing when to stop, and in a misguided attempt to help her feel good about herself, I kept going. "Of course you are!" I said chirpily.

"No, really," she protested. "Sometimes I'm not so good."

I will be forever grateful to this student for challenging me on my mistake, and it was a big one. By referring to her as *good* over and over again, I didn't give her the option of being anything *but* good (at least not around me). But the truth is no one can be *good* all the time, and character is never just one thing. Had I not realized my error, I might have caused her to believe that she could never make mistakes, or that she couldn't make them around me, or that her character was one-dimensional. In short, I could have caused her adopt a fixed mindset about herself.

If we accept that labels such as *smart* and *good* limit how kids see themselves, and contribute to fixed mindsets, then we must also concede that labels such as *bully, victim,* and *bystander* have a similar effect. Dweck's research demonstrates that when children are given the suggestion that a situation is fixed—let's say, if girls are told that they aren't as smart as boys at math, for example—then their (the girls') performance in math suffers. I contend this is also true when it comes to Bully Language, and the effect can be severe, for the *victim* as much as for the *bully.* The case of Eric and Luis illustrates this point.

Eric was branded a bully in the 2nd grade. Eric's behavior wasn't so bad that he got suspended from school, but it was bad enough that he was in the principal's office a lot. Eric had trouble controlling his impulses and expressing his feelings, and occasionally he lashed out in anger at his classmates. During these episodes, he said mean things, and a few of his peers bore the brunt of his bad behavior. One boy in particular, Luis, was deeply affected by Eric's behavior, and he got terribly upset whenever Eric picked on him. When Eric got angry, he would call Luis names, Luis would cry, which made Eric even angrier. To their teachers, Eric was a bully and Luis was a victim, and something had to be done to break the cycle of abuse.

Eric, as a consequence for his behavior, was required to learn about bullying from the school counselor. Together they read a book about bullying that explained how bullies could change. Eric, a bright and generally compliant child, despite his difficulties, waded dutifully through this information, becoming more agitated and glum as he proceeded. Eric's principal and teachers were encouraged by his reaction and took it as a good sign. *Great,* they thought, *he's finally getting it.* What the staff at Eric's school didn't realize, though, was that Eric's agitation and glumness were expressions of shame and helplessness, not remorse. The more he took on the label of bully, the more helpless he felt, because he was being asked to adopt a fixed mindset about himself.

Everyone believed that Eric's redemption hinged upon him accepting the fact that he was a bully, much as a heavy drinker must accept the label of *alcoholic* before true sobriety can being (*Hi, my name is Eric, and I'm a Bully*). But this reasoning did not produce the desired effect. If anything, Eric's behavior became worse because he felt paralyzed by this new definition of himself, the same way smart kids can feel paralyzed when they're called smart all the time. In addition, Eric was confused—what was he supposed to do now? Even if his behavior improved, and he wasn't quite sure how this would happen (in part, because he was 7 years old), he felt ashamed and scared. What if he made a mistake again? What kind of a monster would he be then?

Luis, on the other hand, became acquainted with bully labels from the other end of the stick—as the victim—and he enjoyed certain benefits as a result. First, he wasn't asked to reflect upon any aspect of his behavior, or his reactions to Eric. He only had to consider the role he played in the dynamic as a victim, never as simply one child reacting to another.

Second, Luis was given a lot of sympathy and attention, so much so that he began to wonder whether he could get this much attention for being his regular self. Everyone around him seemed sensitive to his reactions—especially his parents—and they asked him often how he felt. Luis knew he had been the victim of bullying, and he knew this was bad, and so he became extremely attuned to his bad moods and negative mental states. When he felt a negative emotion, be began to fret over the cause and often assigned blame to others. Over time, Luis felt less in control of his emotional states than he had before, and he became more reliant on adults to soothe him when he was upset. The relief he felt when Eric got in trouble was short-lived and was replaced by a sense that nothing had really changed.

Neither Eric nor Luis felt empowered after being assigned the labels *bully* and *victim*, nor did they demonstrate any true learning about themselves or the situation. Eric felt deflated and Luis felt weak, and they both moved forward with a sense of diminishment. Each boy felt stuck in his own way, and branded by the adults around them.

This is the inevitable result of the fixed mindset, and this is what Bully Language creates. It is important to note, however, that I'm not suggesting we do nothing in situations like this. I'm also not suggesting we feel sympathy for Eric's behavior or disregard for Luis' feelings. But the way we choose to think about them, name them, and respond to them makes all the difference in the world. We can just as easily adopt a growth mindset as we can a fixed one when we deal with childhood aggression, and I will explain how we can do this in Chapter 4.

In conclusion, Bully Language is not the most effective way to help children learn from their mistakes, deal with their feelings, or develop new behavior. The conceptual framework that arises from the use of this language keeps us feeling stuck at best, and victimized and shamed at worst. Even in cases where aggression between children is extreme (and I have not used extreme cases as examples in this chapter), Bully Language does not promote the kind of growth and development we want to see in children. And we must remember that we're dealing with children here, young people whose brains are not yet fully developed and whose potential has yet to be realized. When children are labeled we lose sight of the fact that they change constantly and learn easily, and that our impressions of them, as communicated through labels, stay with them for a long time, possibly forever.

So, when does a bully stop being a bully?

When he or she stops being called a bully.

CHAPTER 2

THE DEFINITION OF BULLYING INHIBITS RESILIENCE

OUR CURRENT DEFINITION OF BULLYING is extremely broad and now includes many behaviors that until recently were not thought of as bullying. This sends children the message that they should label and respond with alarm to a vast array of social situations, and that victimhood is practically inevitable in social relationships. In defining so many behaviors as bullying, kids learn that many of their feelings of distress are inherently dangerous and harmful, and that there is something wrong in the routine, albeit painful, struggles they experience at the hands of their peers.

In addition, the broad definition of bullying scares parents, which in turn scares children, and gives the impression that intense and unpleasant social hardships cause only damage. The struggles that now come under the umbrella of bullying serve to empower children mostly in their claims to being victims. In this way, the commonly accepted definition of bullying promotes victimhood, not resilience, and this is terribly problematic considering that resilience is an essential ingredient for success in life.

The New Definition of Bullying

Bullying looks much different now than it did a generation ago. When I began my career working in schools in the late 1980s, school anti-bullying policies were rare and there were no state laws making bullying a crime.

Now, most schools and states have implemented rules and laws against bullying, and those that haven't are in the minority. Back then there were only a few books or scholarly articles available on the topic since bullying wasn't a subject of widespread interest. Currently, though, bullying is a topic of intense scrutiny, and our cultural focus on it has caused us to pay particular attention to its definition.

The original definition of bullying was very specific, and it hinged upon the notion of coercion. (By original I mean the definition in common use before the anti-bullying movement got fully underway, before about 2000: in other words, the definition of bullying in the dictionary). According to this definition, to bully means to coerce another into doing something he/she doesn't want to do, and this coercion is intentional, meaning the bully knows what he's doing. A bully by this standard uses his or her power to intimidate or harm, and by definition the victim is someone who is weaker or has less power or status. Bullying by this definition is an act that usually involves physical intimidation or threats—violence is the bully's calling card. Things have changed.

Now, according to the Department of Health and Human Services, bullying includes such behaviors as "making mean or rude gestures," "spitting," "spreading rumors," and "leaving someone out on purpose."[1] I first realized our definition of bullying had changed when I stumbled upon an article about bullying in schools in a professional journal. Shivers went down my spine when I read that over half of all students surveyed claimed that they'd been bullied or had witnessed bullying at school. I admit I was shocked by the statistics—they described a veritable explosion of menacing behaviors. I was also alarmed that I hadn't seen this explosion in the schools where I'd worked and consulted. It seems I had missed this dangerous epidemic. I felt a lump in my throat as I imagined all of the things I had overlooked in the hallways at school—all the damage that was being done right under my nose. How could I have been so blind?

Then I read the definition of bullying used by the authors. That's when I got a sense that it wasn't just the number of incidents of bullying that had changed, but also the definition. The article stated that bullying now

---

1. www.stopbullying.gov

included many behaviors not formerly considered as such, things such as name-calling and teasing. Most of the garden-variety mean behaviors that are rampant in schools and throughout childhood (and adulthood, if we're going to be honest about it), were now included in the list. It appeared as though, all of a sudden, our culture (or at least the authors of the study) had made a determination that some formerly acceptable, although hurtful, behaviors were now truly harmful, and that they now constituted bullying.

This broader definition of bullying is now well accepted, as the Department of Health and Human Services definition attests, but at the time I read this article, it was new—and news—to me. Bullying now constitutes a wide range of behaviors, and coercion, physical contact or threats of violence do not necessarily come into play. Depending on the specific anti-bullying policy, bullying is characterized as being either physical, emotional, or verbal, or as deriving from harassment based on specific things such as race, gender, sexual orientation, religion, ethnicity, etc. In addition, bullying via electronic media—texting, e-mail, etc.—i.e. cyber-bullying, is now included in the definition. As is clear, bullying can take many forms according to the current standards, but what's noteworthy is the inclusion of emotional bullying, which simply wasn't in our cultural consciousness a generation ago.[2]

According to one school's policies, emotional bullying includes "being unfriendly (e.g. hiding books), threatening gestures, spreading rumors, excluding someone from groups," and, according to another's, "teasing, putdowns, name-calling, threatening looks, social isolation." The bully in these cases uses emotional or psychological tactics, rather than physical might, to harm the victim. And this is where things get more complicated. What does emotional bullying actually look like? This is a critical question to understand for parents and those who work with kids and who are charged with keeping them safe. Emotional bullying is much more subtle than physical bullying, and therefore much more open to interpretation. Most people are pretty clear about what physical

---

2. I encourage you to investigate your local school and state government anti-bullying policies. I have not spelled out specific policies here because they are all a little different (although many school districts and states have general templates that individual schools adopt).

bullying looks like (which is why I believe many articles on bullying feature photographs showing a big kid pummeling a smaller one—it's an easy concept to capture). But emotional bullying isn't always as clear.

For instance, when it comes to social isolation or exclusion, this might look like willfully preventing someone from joining a game at recess, or from sitting at a particular table in the cafeteria. Imagine a child searching for a place to sit to eat lunch, seeing an empty seat at a table populated with her classmates, and approaching the table with the intention of joining the group only to discover that the girls—upon seeing her approach—have filled the empty seat with a backpack, thus preventing her from taking a seat. Words may not be spoken, but the message is clear: you're not welcome here.

It gets even more subtle. Consider the issue of threatening looks. Imagine two middle school girls walking down the hallway at school. They see a classmate approaching from the other direction. As they pass the classmate the girls roll their eyes contemptuously at her, and whisper and laugh as they continue down the hallway. As you can see, coercion isn't part of the picture in either of the above examples. Sure, the girl in the cafeteria is prevented from sitting with her classmates, and therefore she's coerced into sitting elsewhere, but coercion isn't the primary goal of the perpetrators, exclusion is. And in the second example, who knows what the goal of the behavior is? Humiliation, rejection, or just being mean? It's difficult to say, but according to the current definition, both of the examples above could qualify as bullying.

Emotional bullying is much harder to identify and monitor than physical bullying is, for obvious reasons. Physical bullying can leave evidence, and it can be witnessed and understood without the need for (much) interpretation. A bigger kid repeatedly beats up a smaller one in the schoolyard and it's pretty clear what's going on. But when a child is excluded from the table at lunchtime? There could be numerous explanations; maybe there just wasn't a seat available.

In order for the negative behaviors to reach the threshold of bullying, they must be repeated—you haven't been bullied if you've been denied a seat at the table just once. Bullying, therefore, is not a specific event but rather a pattern of behavior that is aggressive, intentional or deliberately hostile. How often the behavior must be repeated in order for it to constitute bullying is not specified in anti-bullying policies, and this points to one of the many challenges we face in dealing with bullying. If name-calling happens once it's not bullying, but twice? When does the behavior become a pattern? Three times?

Maybe bad behavior crosses the line into bullying when a child starts to feel distressed. But what if two children are subjected to the same treatment and one feels terrible after two episodes but the other doesn't feel bad at all? Has only one child been bullied, or both of them, or neither? Common sense would say that's a judgment call, but whose call is it and upon whose judgment do we rely, the victim's, the person the victim reports it to, the parents or teachers of the victim, a bystander? Who gets to determine when bullying has occurred?

As you can see, there are many implications to the new definition of bullying, and determining whether bullying has occurred is not as simple as it might seem at first, but one thing is clear. The new definition guarantees that we will see bullying everywhere, and this fact has changed our perception of children and childhood. When phrases such as *schoolyard tyranny* and *schoolyard battlefield* are used in anti-bullying books to describe the experience of childhood, we can be certain the new definition of bullying has permeated our culture and that we're running scared.[3]

Bullying Statistics, Jerrymandering, and the Issue of Self-Reporting

Many studies claim that bullying is happening everywhere, practically around the clock.[4] There's been an explosion of new and dangerous behavior, or at least that's what the statistics would have us believe. But the behavior in question is neither new nor dangerous (in most cases), and yet we have worked ourselves into a veritable frenzy over it.

The explosion we're seeing in bullying is due to our expanded definition of it, not to a shift in behavior, and this fact alone should serve to calm us all down. We are not facing an elevated threat—a new demon simply isn't there. What we're seeing now is what has always been there, but it has been repackaged and reissued and rebranded in an advertising

3. Search for the titles of anti-bullying books to see this.

4. Bullystatistics.org

campaign (in the form of anti-bullying workshops, websites, initiatives, alarming new reports, etc.) that comes with a lot of statistics to support its new image. The statistics that suggest bullying is a major threat to our children are nothing more than the redrawing of boundaries of aggression—a jerrymandering of negative childhood behavior. To jerrymander is to redraw the lines of political districts with the intent of creating a more favorable outcome for one or another political party. This is what has happened with the definition of bullying. The districts have been redrawn—that is, the definition has been expanded, such that now it fits into fear-based assumptions of childhood. Because so many behaviors are now included in the bully "district," the statistics serve to support the belief that we should fear what's happening among children.

This reconfiguration of childhood aggression has been extremely successful in convincing many of us that a new threat exists, and this new boundary fairly dominates the scene when it comes to concerns about childhood. But this statistical method of redistricting should be examined critically before it is accepted as truth; if we don't pay attention soon we will get stuck in this new bully territory.

If you do a little research on the statistics on bullying you will discover two things. First, that the statistics are remarkably inconsistent, and second, that much of the data comes from the same few studies, which then get recycled from anti-bullying website to blogger to newspaper article to anti-bullying education materials to magazine article to newscast and finally back to anti-bullying website. There's not a tremendous amount out there, but what's there gets used over and over again, which makes the data seem both hefty and pervasive. It's not.

Let's say you want some information about bullying, so you decide to do some research on the Internet. You visit one website and find some statistics that alarm you. You decide you better learn more—*this is serious stuff!* So you travel to another website—again, more statistics, maybe packaged a little differently, with different commentary, and your alarm increases. Then you read an article about bullying in your local newspaper and think, *this is everywhere—even in my hometown—yikes!* This leads you to investigate some more. You visit site after site, getting more and more frightened as you proceed, but just because you've been all over the Internet doesn't mean that you're actually getting more or different information. You're not; you're getting the same information over and over again, and this creates an indelible impression that real damage is occurring all over the place, all the time, and to everyone. This just isn't the case.

All of this says less about childhood aggression than it does about media aggressiveness and how repeated exposure to the same information creates a false impression of danger. It works: we're scared, and the recycled statistics, measuring things that didn't scare us a generation ago, but which have been jerrymandered into our boundaries of alarm, now have many of us in a frenzy.

Many people are now tuned in to bullying and are scared, because regardless of whether the data is inconsistent and not that robust, they claim to describe danger to children, and danger to children is an inherently scary topic. As such, the scary details increase fear, and once people get scared they assume the scary details must be true because they support their feelings. When this happens, critical thinking tends to fly out the window. Once critical thinking is abandoned, and once feelings become the primary guide to inform opinions and reactions, we're in trouble as a culture. This is the precipice upon which we stand now when it comes to childhood aggression.

The good news is that we can pay attention to the information we're receiving *and* keep our wits about us, and here's why. Just a little digging reveals that the data really isn't that scary, and the issue of self-reporting is the primary reason.

Many studies on bullying use a methodology that employs self-reporting, which means subjects (in this case, children) are asked questions about their behavior or about what's happened to them, and their answers constitute the results. In addition, many studies ask children not only if they've been bullied but also if they have observed or know of others getting bullied. This contributes to a large degree to the ballooning of the statistics because it means every child can theoretically answer *yes* to having observed others being bullied but be referring to the same incident or case. With this methodology, bullying is rampant.

Factor into this methodology the expanded definition of bullying and you can see where this is headed. Ask children, especially middle-school children, if they have been teased, excluded, called names, etc.—or if they have observed others being teased, excluded, or called names, etc.—and you're going to get a mountain of data. Suddenly you have an epidemic on your hands. Plus, when this data is considered in isolation, all of the good things that happen to children get ignored—how often they laugh with friends, have fun playing games, do kind things for one another. It's as though a survey is taken of rainy days and the sunshine that inevitably follows isn't factored in. No one is asking children about what's good in their world. This leads to an incredibly skewed perspective of childhood, and it contributes considerably to our cultural alarm.

If we look for trouble, then we'll surely find it, and if we look *only* for trouble, then trouble is the only thing we'll find. This is the current method when it comes to determining what's happening with children. They are asked very specific, negative questions about their experience with their peers, such as: *do you feel bad, what's wrong, are you hurt, who hurt you, did other people get hurt?* Absent from this type of survey are questions such as: *what's going well, what's right, where are you succeeding, who do you like, who likes you?* The results would be very different if children were asked these sorts of questions, and no doubt a very different impression of childhood would emerge. When children are asked questions that frame their social lives as potentially dangerous, then guess what? That's the information they'll deliver back, and that's what we (and they) will see and believe to be true.

One study commissioned by CNN, which described aggressive behavior among teenagers as *social combat*, surveyed more than 700 students at one high school, and asked them questions about aggressive behavior. "The students were also given a roster of the entire school in which every student had an identification number and kids were asked to write down specifically who did what."[5]

To repeat: the kids were asked to report *who did what!* I wish someone had given me a survey like this in high school. I would have relished the opportunity to rat out every kid I didn't like and whom I thought had treated me badly. And no doubt there would have been plenty of kids who would have relished the opportunity to do the same thing to me. Did the researchers factor in the survey itself as a form of *social combat*? What a

5. www.cnn.com/2011/10/10/us/ac-360-bullying-study/index.html

way to increase hostility among the troops, and they administered it four times during the school year. *Four times.*

I'll make you a bet that the survey was the only assignment every single kid successfully completed that year. *Forget about Algebra class— let's take that social combat survey again!* And then to be on national television to talk about the results—and to tell the whole world about the heartless bullies in your school, and to be able to identify them—does it get any better than this? Self-righteousness and revenge are even sweeter when they're broadcast nationwide. Clearly the researchers knew nothing about teenagers. This is a teenager's dream come true—to rate each other on degrees of meanness and then to sit back and point the finger. The researchers gave it to them on a silver platter, and now we're expected to fret over it. This is crazy!

Nevertheless, it's from these kinds of studies that data about bullying is being culled: from kids, about themselves, about other kids, and about behavior that has existed since the dawn of time. Now that the behavior has been reconfigured as dangerous and worthy of prime time attention, *social combat*, kids are being told again and again that they're being victimized, so they must rate each other on a scale to identify who's doing what to whom. If this isn't stirring the pot, what is?

Another area where the statistics are misleading is bullying and suicide. One anti-bullying website claims that a child commits suicide due to bullying very 30 minutes.[6] I decided to do the math to determine what this translates into per year. That's two suicides per hour, multiplied by 24 (hours), times 365 (days), which equals 17,520 suicides per year due to bullying (2x24x365=17,520).

This seemed high so I looked up the total number of childhood suicides per year and discovered that the numbers are about equal. This means that some anti-bullying advocates are claiming the maximum number of childhood suicides for themselves. Numbers not withstanding, it can be very difficult to determine the cause of suicide. As one suicide prevention expert explains, "In suicide prevention, we tend to favor the explanation that there are multiple causes."[7] What we do know is that

---

6. www.safevilleusa.com/safecircles/home

7. Ann Haas, a senior project specialist with the American Foundation for

most teens who commit suicide have a psychiatric condition, such as depression and anxiety, present at the time of death, and therefore it's simply not possible to connect all of these deaths solely to bullying.

Anti-bullying activists are not putting forth these numbers or using such inventive methodology to purposely confuse or mislead us. I believe they are as legitimately concerned about children as the rest of us. But this doesn't excuse or justify creating studies that generate a view of childhood that is imbalanced, inflammatory, and deceptive.

This is our current zeitgeist, that we are in the midst of an epidemic of bullying and that childhood is an incredibly dangerous proposition.

The New Definition of Bullying and Retroactive Victimization

The new definition of bullying also means adults can reminisce about their own childhood struggles, label it as bullying, and retroactively lay claim to victimhood. This trend can be charted by listening to our celebrities, many of whom have embraced the anti-bullying cause wholeheartedly while simultaneously telling tales of their own victimization.[8] Celebrity stories of woe have done as much as anything to educate us about the expanded definition of bullying, in addition to assuring us that the new definition—and the problem of bullying—is here to stay.

This celebrity trend also points to the widely accepted belief that victimhood confers upon the bearer some measure of authenticity, and perhaps even status. Why else would you blab about it on a blog? Suffering at the hands of others—and being completely blameless and taking no responsibility for what happened—is now a badge of honor, and bestows upon the victim a license to feel self-righteous and point the finger in

---

Suicide Prevention, quoted in the *Huffington Post*, February 12, 2012, www. huffingtonpost.com/2012/02/08/bullying-suicide-teens-depression_n_1247875. html

8. The names of the celebrities are not provided because their actual identities aren't important. What's important is that famous people are on websites (their own and anti-bullying ones) claiming their victimhood, and usually for things that underscore how broad and overarching our definition of bullying has become. All references cited here come from Bullyville.com.

return and, in the case of celebrities, to get a lot of publicity at the same time.

For example, one celebrity, a woman now in her mid-twenties, describes on one anti-bullying website how she was targeted in high school by a girl "gang." She said, "I was with a big group of friends when this girl I hardly knew came up to me and said, 'You don't belong here—these people aren't your friends.' Well, I'm the most sensitive person, so I just burst into tears in front of everyone. I ran to the bathroom crying. Girls can be so nasty." She then added, "I've realized girls who do stuff like that will never amount to anything in life. They reach their peak at high school, then that's it—they don't go anywhere."

Another actor discusses how difficult it was for him being shorter than everyone else—even the girls—during high school. He also suffered because his name rhymes with another word and thus he was saddled with a nickname throughout high school (which, by the way, was not a profanity or a putdown, just a nickname). Another celebrity was bullied for having red hair, another for wearing "nerdy" glasses, and yet another for having a big nose and being fat. The litany of complaints seems endless, and one reality show "star" warns readers that bullying never stops—*there are even bullies in adulthood!*

The banner over all of these testimonials reads *Bullying Survivor.*

In addition to the celebrity stories, readers on one particular anti-bullying/bullying awareness website are invited to share their own narratives. Common themes that run through the stories are *I am different, no one understands me, everyone's against me* and *I'm the only one who's nice/sensitive/caring,* and then these feelings are tied to the behavior of others, as in *I feel this way because I was bullied.*

But here's the rub: the feelings expressed in most of the testimonials are common and typical during adolescence. Adolescence is a time when feelings of alienation, confusion, and being painfully different prevail (more on this in Chapter 3); most adolescents don't jump out of bed each morning full of confidence. The anti-bullying movement seems to have lost sight of this fact. Now they're teaching kids that there's something inherently wrong with these feelings (which is not to say these feelings aren't awful to deal with). Teenagers live in the hot house of adolescence, and they bump up against each other all the time. All of them feel self-conscious and ugly and moody at times, which means that they behave in short-tempered, selfish, and unkind ways at times. When this situation reaches a certain threshold—as it inevitably does—it's now called bullying, and kids are being taught that it's dangerous and shouldn't happen.

I am not suggesting people who claim to have been bullied didn't have negative interactions with their peers and feel great pain as a result; no doubt they did. But the expanded definition of bullying now provides an explanation for their experiences of pain that may not explain the whole story. On some days, to be an adolescent is to be bullied by life and it can really be that hard and overwhelming, even without a classmate calling you fat.

This is what kids are being taught in light of the expanded definition of bullying:

1. The potential for victimization is everywhere.

2. Your pain and insecurities are probably a result of the meanness of others.

3. You should never have to feel this way—life should be smooth sailing from ages 10 to 20.

4. You can/should hold onto your pain—there is no statute of limitations on claiming victimhood.

How did we get here as a culture? How did we get to the point where being teased for wearing glasses (or having red hair or being short or fat or nerdy) is a form of persecution that brings with it the potential for lasting harm and perpetual claims to victimization?

As mentioned, our cultural attention to bullying is a recent development. Nobody talked about bullying as being a serious problem a generation ago. It simply wasn't on the radar screen. Some might argue that this is because we were ignoring the problem, but it's more complicated than that. Certainly kids had issues with each other back then, but there's no research to suggest that these issues were substantially different than what kids deal with now. In fact, some research indicates that childhood has never been safer, despite all the statistics about bullying.[9] It stands to reason, then, that something significant happened in the past few decades

---

9. National Center for Educational Statistics, nces.ed.gov

to make many of us so fearful of childhood aggression and what goes on between children, and to make bullying, as one self-proclaimed expert in the field says, "*the* problem of our day."

That something was Columbine.

Columbine: The Turning Point

On Tuesday, April 20, 1999, Eric Harris and Dylan Klebold, seniors at Columbine High School in Littleton Colorado, outside of Denver, planted bombs in their school cafeteria. Their plan was to detonate the devices at lunchtime and kill as many of their classmates as possible (their hope was to kill hundreds). The boys' preparations were extensive and calculating. At the appointed hour, they positioned themselves in the student parking lot, near one of the school entrances, and waited for the bombs to go off. From their outdoor perches they planned to shoot classmates as they fled the firestorm. The boys wanted to see the terror on their classmates' faces as they attempted to escape the chaos created by the bombs' explosions and take out as many survivors as possible as they ran for safety.

Luckily, the bombs failed to detonate and mass destruction was avoided, but when Eric and Dylan realized their bombs were duds they stormed the school and rampaged for about an hour, randomly shooting and terrorizing students and faculty. In the end, the boys killed 12 students and one teacher before killing themselves.

What made Columbine such a traumatizing and significant event for the nation, beyond the obvious facts, was that it played out in real time in the media. Almost as soon as Eric and Dylan started their rampage, terrified teachers and students—many of them holed up inside the school in classrooms, closets, and the library—used cell phones to contact their families, 911, and the local Denver TV stations. As a result, television crews were on the scene almost immediately, and reporters and news anchors were able to broadcast live conversations with terrorized captives hiding inside the school building, while Eric and Dylan were still at large. Americans watching TV that day bore witness to the horror as it was happening, and did so from the perspective of the victims. (It is interesting to note that cell phone use was not yet widespread in 1999; Columbine was perhaps the first massive traumatic event where cell phones played a key role in communicating information. Our understanding of the trag-edy was made possible, in part, by cell phones, and they gave the average American a degree of connection to the event that would not have been possible only a few years earlier.)

Naturally, the nation was captivated by the images and voices of trau-matized and hysterical students that were broadcast repeatedly—the dra-matic rescue of a student from the window of the school library being a horrifying, and much replayed, highlight. Even students trapped inside the school watched the events unfold on televisions in the classrooms; they got their information about what was happening from the media, just like the rest of us did.

Understandably, the media coverage of the massacre was extensive, and Americans were riveted by the unfolding terror. And the search for answers began almost immediately. Once the events had been chronicled (and replayed again and again), the focus of the story shifted from *what* had happened to *why*. Everyone wanted to know about Eric Harris and Dylan Klebold. Who were these boys? What made them do what they did? It seemed so inexplicable. What could cause two kids from good families, living the American dream in suburban Colorado, to unleash such destruction on their fellow students? How could this have happened to such nice kids in such a nice place?

The public demanded answers to these questions, and the media was happy to oblige. As a result, before any real investigations were con-ducted, before forensics teams had the chance to scour the scene (and search the perpetrators' homes and read their detailed journals), and before the myriad of evidence was evaluated, idle speculation morphed into theory, which then hardened into fact, and America had the answer it was looking for.

Bullying.

Eric and Dylan had been bullied, the media proclaimed, which is why they almost blew up their school, killed as many people as they could, and then committed suicide. Within hours of the massacre, stories to sup-port this theory started to emerge. According to sources (who were often students who didn't know the boys), Eric and Dylan were part of a group called the Trench Coat Mafia (a reference to the trench coats they occa-sionally wore and had donned on the day of the shootings), a group that existed on the periphery of the allegedly harsh, exclusive, and socially stratified world that was Columbine High. Members of this group were misunderstood outsiders, the media reported, forever denied access to the world of social privilege enjoyed by the "insiders" at the school—the jocks, the mean girls, the rich kids, and the other menacing social leaders who roamed the school halls prowling for victims.

According to reports, Eric and Dylan were picked on, castigated, and disdained by their peers because they were weird and different. As members of the Trench Coat Mafia, they suffered mightily at the hands of the socially powerful in-crowd at Columbine, and the bullying was relentless.

Almost as soon as the media offered this motive for *Columbine*—as the massacre quickly became known—it was accepted as truth, and the rallying cries began. *No more bullying!* parents demanded. *Zero tolerance for bullies!* teachers declared. From the moment the dust settled in the hallways of the school, Bully Nation (the term I use for the anti-bully movement) was born, and echoes of these original cries can still be heard in every schoolyard, classroom, playground, and daycare center across America.

At the time, the connections drawn between Columbine and bullying were so strong and convincing that they weren't challenged for years, and by the time they were, our approach to childhood aggression had permanently changed. After Columbine, most Americans became convinced on some level that bullying was so rampant and pernicious that a massacre like Columbine was inevitable and even understandable—albeit inappropriate—given the trials suffered by victims like Eric and Dylan.[10]

An essential takeaway at the time of Columbine was that bullying was a scourge sweeping the nation and that it must be taken seriously and

---

10. The theory that Eric and Dylan were bullied was so well accepted that it even made it onto the big screen, in the movie *Bowling for Columbine* (2002). There is a scene where director Michael Moore interviews Matt Stone, one of the co-creators of the television show South Park and a native of Littleton, Colorado. In a voiceover, Moore says, "Matt . . . found a way to take [his] anger at being different in Littleton and turn it, not into carnage [like Eric and Dylan], but into a cartoon [South Park]." Matt then explains that all of the "dorks" in high school went on to do interesting things while all the cool kids are still in Littleton, selling insurance. "I wish someone could have grabbed them [Eric and Dylan]." Matt says. "If someone could have told them that, then maybe they wouldn't have done it."

stopped, of course. If bullying could cause the tragedy at Columbine, the reasoning went, then such massacres could happen anywhere. Many in the anti-bullying movement continue to contend that if we're not vigilant about bullying, then tragedies of this nature will continue to occur. And thus the call to action carries on.

Thanks in part to Columbine, and as a result of the expanded definition of bullying, we now see it everywhere, and lots of us are terrified. The cultural belief is that aggression between children is necessarily and inevitably harmful, and that children may not be safe with their peers in school or have adequate resilience to get through childhood without emotional damage. Anti-bullying rhetoric would have us accept, as fact, that our way of thinking about childhood aggression—in the form of Bully Language and labels, or the fixed mindset—is both appropriate and accurate, and that fear and hyper-vigilance are the best responses to the pains and challenges of childhood.

From my perspective, working in the field with children, it was Columbine that got this ball rolling. It was the seminal expression of childhood aggression of our generation, and it changed the cultural perspective in profound ways. This makes sense. There was no way to experience Columbine—up close and personal, thanks to the media—and not feel terrified and transformed forever as a result. America did not overreact to the tragedy as it was delivered and explained at the time. Columbine left many questions in its wake, and bullying was the most convenient answer at the time.

In the country's desire to comprehend the incomprehensible and regain a sense of control, bullying became the explanation of choice for Eric and Dylan's behavior—not severe psychopathology, which in fact was the main culprit, or easy access to guns and ammunition, which made the tragedy possible.[11] No, the problem was bullying. And I think this helped

---

11. Mental health experts agreed years later that Eric Harris suffered from Anti-Social Personality Disorder; he was a sociopath. Eric's voluminous journals provided investigators with an in-depth view into the mind of a sociopath (also known as psychopath). Anti-Social Personality Disorder is characterized by, among other things, lack of empathy, remorse, shame or guilt; pathological lying; shallow emotions; grandiose sense of self and extreme narcissism; superficial charm; trouble with the law. Eric had all of these in spades, and he carefully

the country move on, at least initially. *Great,* we said with a sigh of relief, *at least we have a reason for the disaster. Now we can make sure it doesn't happen again.* An enemy had been identified, and it was bullying. But did we get it right?

As it happened, a crucial fact got overlooked in the aftermath of the massacre, a fact that changed the course of bully history forever: Eric and Dylan weren't the victims of bullying. It turns out Columbine had nothing to do with bullying.[12] Eric and Dylan weren't mistreated or marginalized by their peers, nor were they subjected to repeated abuse. In addition, Columbine High School wasn't a dysfunctional community rife with mean and terrible kids, a veritable breeding ground for aggression.

For weeks and months after the massacre, the media portrayed Columbine as an alarmingly dysfunctional community, but it wasn't. By all accounts it was a caring, responsive school, and it fostered no more problematic behavior than any other school in America. But this didn't come to light until much later. It wasn't until years after the massacre that investigators understood Eric and Dylan's motives. It took time for all of the pieces of the puzzle to fall into place, and for investigators to realize that the boys did what they did for complex reasons, bullying not being one of them.

Nevertheless, by the time the truth came to light the Myth of Columbine was set in stone, and bullying was on its way to being perceived as one of the biggest threats facing America's children. Some might argue that the facts about the cause of Columbine don't matter at this point, because the myth has become part of our collective truth.

In the end, Columbine put bullying on the map and it put America on high alert.

---

planned his violent rampage for over a year. Dylan, on the other hand, was lost. He wouldn't have come up with the plan for Columbine on his own, but he was depressed and suicidal enough to sign on. (Sociopaths are rare, and most sociopaths are not violent. Instead of killing people like Eric Harris did, non-violent sociopaths may be quite high-functioning and they generally skirt the law. If they're very successful, non-violent sociopaths might engage in high brow criminal activity, such as running corporations in Enron fashion or bilking people of their life savings, like Bernie Madoff.)

12. I am indebted to Dave Cullen and his excellent book *Columbine* (Twelve, March 2010) for this information.

Fear: The Legacy of Columbine

Changes occurred in schools after Columbine. Teachers searched for any indication of violence in their students' behavior, including their writing, speech, or artwork. Any signs of distress, or perceived distress, were dealt with swiftly (although not necessarily effectively). Teachers wondered how they could determine whether the next Eric or Dylan was sitting in their classroom. How could they prevent the next tragedy from happening? Parents were fearful, too. Would their children be safe at school, and how could they protect kids from their dangerous classmates?

People were scared.

I remember the case of one boy, a 16-year-old high school junior, whose entries in his English journal a few months after Columbine raised some red flags. He had used some violent imagery to express his feelings, which left his teacher in a panic. She went to the chair of her department, who went to the vice principal, who went to the principal, who went to the child's parent. People were scared out of their minds that this boy had been hurt and was now in danger of hurting himself or others. The school wanted him to undergo a psychiatric evaluation, which the student himself thought was ridiculous. When confronted with everyone's concern, the boy claimed he had merely been blowing off some steam.

Before Columbine, interventions like this were rare. I had not heard of anything like this before the massacre; now such interventions are routine. And rightly so—we should *always* respond if we fear a child is in danger. But what constitutes true danger? With our new definition of bullying, our conception of what is dangerous has expanded considerably. Now, per the definition, teasing is dangerous. Name-calling is dangerous. Being excluded from a game at recess is dangerous. No wonder people are scared.

After Columbine, the fear seemed justified. Contemplating the connection between bullying and wanton murder was terrifying, but it was a reasonable connection to make given how the media portrayed the tragedy. Years after Columbine many of us are still terrified, despite the fact that the massacre had nothing to do with bullying. And while we might not be consciously terrified of another Columbine occurring, we're unabashedly, and increasingly, terrified of bullying. Bullying now tops the list of things parents are scared of. A national survey commissioned by Care.com, in October 2010, reported that, "Nearly one in three parents of children ages 12-17 agree that bullying is a more serious concern than other dangers, including domestic terrorism, car accidents, and suicide."[13]

In the course of just a decade, bullying has gone from being something that was underneath the radar to being the thing parents are most concerned about when it comes to children's welfare. This is truly astonishing given that, as I've said, childhood is safer than ever before by many accounts and measures.[14] If Columbine was the event that sparked this firestorm about bullying, then parents' fears continue to serve as the kindling, and there's nothing to suggest that this fear is going away any time soon. The parents I work with are very worried about bullying, and even when they are presented with facts that should serve to allay their fears, they remain scared. Even when their own children have never been bullied or witnessed bullying themselves, they remain fearful.

I recently heard of a group of parents who get together regularly to discuss "problem kids" in their children's schools. The parents identify the children whom they believe to be actual or potential bullies (I assume their own children do not make the list) and then work to keep their children away from the potential threats. This is what scared looks like, and this fear is both the cause and the effect of our expanded definition of bullying.

I can assure you that the children of the above-mentioned parents live in some of the safest areas of the country; their risk of experiencing physical violence at the hands of their peers is negligible. In truth, these kids are much more likely to experience self-inflicted dangers, such as car accidents, drug or alcohol misuse, or snowboarding into a tree, than physical harm by a classmate. For these concerned parents, then, physical bullying can't be the driving force behind their fears. If physical bullying were our greatest fear as a culture, then the definition of bullying wouldn't have increased the way it has over the past decade. No, the fear isn't about children getting hurt physically, it's about them getting hurt emotionally, and this is what the new definition of bullying is trying to address.

---

13. Care.com, Wednesday, October 20, 2010.

14. National Center for Educational Statistics.

Our cultural concern about children experiencing psychological pain, and the desire to prevent it, are the primary reasons the definition of bullying has expanded beyond recognition. But this has had a paradoxical effect on kids. Instead of promoting the development of resilience, which is presumably the goal of anti-bullying efforts, it actually inhibits it. Why? Think about it. Bullying is everywhere: in the statistics, on the news, in the movies. Wouldn't you be scared if you were a kid? But bullying is everywhere because the definition of bullying has changed, not because children have changed, and not because the risk of pain or damage is any worse than it used to be. The perception is that childhood is more dangerous now because of bullying, but it's not, nevertheless, this is the perception being taught to children, and this *is* dangerous because it affects how children develop resilience.

Resilience

Resilience is the psychological ability to bounce back, overcome adversity, and deal with the many challenges of life. Just as the body has an immune system, the psyche has resilience, and like the immune system, resilience is something we can foster and build in ourselves and in our children. When our resilience is well developed and robust, we can weather all kinds of psychological ups and downs; when our resilience is compromised, we feel weak and get emotionally sick.

It is no exaggeration to say that resilience is *an* essential ingredient for success in life, if not *the* most essential ingredient. Without it, the world seems overwhelming and scary and we limit ourselves at every turn. So, resilience is a must. The good news is that there are plenty of opportunities to develop resilience all around us. We don't need to seek them out, in the same way we don't need to seek out germs to develop our immune system. Germs are all around us, and our exposure to them, in reasonable doses, serves to keep us healthy: so, too, with resilience. Our exposure to challenges, in reasonable doses, keeps us strong and builds our resilience, and the more resilience we build, the more effectively we deal with challenges as we age.

Resilience can also be likened to a muscle that gets exercised throughout life. Anytime we take a test, run a race, try something new, make a friend, lose a friend, get our hearts broken, have a child, apply for a job, or get laid off from a job, we are attempting a challenge and thus giving ourselves the opportunity to build resilience. Any of these challenges can make us stronger—even when they cause us great pain and hardship in the process—or they can defeat us. It all depends on our resilience.

The essence of resilience is simple, and a colleague of mine captured it for me once when she explained, *Just because I lose, it doesn't mean I'm a loser.*[15] My colleague packed a lot of wisdom about resilience into this pithy phrase. First, to develop resilience we have to be tested, which means we have to put ourselves out there, and we risk something in the process (perhaps our pride, our heart, a championship). Second, it's not enough to just put oneself out there. The real measure of resilience comes after-the-fact; it's how we deal with a loss or hardship that both strengthens and demonstrates our resilience. The choice is ours: will our losses defeat and define us, or will they cause us to bounce back even stronger? To lose and to not consider oneself a loser is an expression of true psychological resilience.

Resilience and resistance tend to go hand in hand, and examples of this exist throughout the natural world. In the late 1980s and early 1990s, scientists created something called Biosphere 2, a self-sustaining, natural environment. Biosphere 2 (Earth being Biosphere 1) was a huge enclosure located in the Arizona desert and, somewhat like Noah's ark, it was jam-packed with various species of plant and animal life (plus a few people). The goal was to fill Biosphere 2 with a perfectly balanced set of biological ingredients, seal it up, and let it thrive.

After a few years, scientists examined the data and noticed something interesting: the trees in Biosphere 2 didn't develop to their full potential. They grew rapidly because they were in a protected environment, but they didn't develop strength. At first, this didn't make sense. All of the elements necessary for success had been in place: sunlight, moisture, and whatever else trees need. Except one thing: wind. There was no wind in Biosphere 2, and it turns out trees need wind in order to thrive.

Without wind, trees don't have any resistance—they have nothing to push against—and resistance is what helps them develop strength and

---

15. Thanks to Anne Travis Brownley for being such a model of resilient thinking.

resilience. Wind is the critical element trees need in order to develop their tree muscles, so to speak, and while they still grow without it, they don't grow strong. Whereas the trees of Biosphere 2 may not provide the perfect analogy, it is fair to say that people also need resistance to develop strength and resilience, and that such resistance comes in the form of challenges, obstacles, and even setbacks and episodic hardship—this is our wind.

Children need to face many challenges if they want to develop resilience, but the new definition of bullying communicates to children that many of these challenges will serve to break them down rather than build them up in the long run. Make no mistake, kids pay attention, and they are paying attention to what is being said about bullying. What is being communicated is going to stick with them and determine how they see themselves and how they respond to each other. The current definition of bullying teaches children that when they are hurt they are victims, that many of the negative interactions they have with their peers can cause damage, and that their negative feelings can be harmful. In an effort to keep children feeling safe, the current definition of bullying has instead made almost every negative social interaction a potential danger, which threatens to inhibit children's capacity to develop and increase a sense of resilience.

The Path of Least Resilience

If we return to our celebrity victims for a moment we can see how this lesson gets communicated. Let's take the case of the woman who was targeted by a girl "gang." She said "I was with a big group of friends when this girl I hardly knew came up to me and said, 'You don't belong here—these people aren't your friends.' Well, I'm the most sensitive person, so I just burst into tears in front of everyone. I ran to the bathroom crying. Girls can be so nasty." Over time, she came to believe that, "Girls who do stuff like that will never amount to anything in life. They reach their peak at high school, then that's it—they don't go anywhere."

This narrative, while mild, exemplifies what many people today consider to be bullying: someone feels attacked, has a painful emotional reaction as a result, and believes her attackers have willfully caused her pain and that they should be damned for it. But taking a closer look at this scenario we can see how our celebrity had choices about how she interpreted

and reacted to the situation, and that—with the support and encouragement of our anti-bullying hysteria—she took what I call the Path of Least
Resilience at every turn. We walk the Path of Least Resilience when we
choose to interpret a situation in a negative light, refuse to see the positive
aspects that exist, take no responsibility for our feelings and reactions,
and hang on to negativity and pain long after-the-fact. As we shall see,
our celebrity walked straight down this Path.

Step 1: *I was with a big group of friends.* By her own account, our
celebrity had friends, and lots of them. She was clearly hanging out with
these friends at school, so she had a support system. However, her takeaway down the Path of Least Resilience was that the world was against her
(this is the adolescent brain in action).

Step 2: *When this girl I hardly knew came up to me and said, "You don't
belong here—these people aren't your friends."* Again, by our celebrity's
account, the offending girl (who was earlier described as a "gang") was
someone she hardly knew. Our celebrity was knocked off-center by someone she hardly knew who presumably, and by definition, wouldn't really
be in a position to render judgment on her status among her friends.
Nevertheless, our celebrity's takeaway was to feel incredibly wounded by
the statement.

Step 3: *Well, I'm the most sensitive person, so I just burst into tears in
front of everyone. I ran to the bathroom crying.* This is not an abnormal
reaction for teens, especially girls. She felt hurt by what the semi-stranger
had said, embarrassed by her reaction, and clearly overwhelmed, so she
tried to escape the situation by rushing to the bathroom—all normal
reactions during adolescence. But adolescents have a hard time understanding this in the moment—that their reactions are often overreac-
tions. By her own admission, our celebrity was *the most sensitive person,*
however she didn't factor this into her analysis of the situation. She had
information available to her that was evidence of her tendency for overreaction but she used it as proof of malice and wrongdoing on the part of
her attacker.

Step 4: *Girls can be so nasty. Girls who do stuff like that will never
amount to anything in life. They reach their peak at high school, then that's
it—they don't go anywhere.* In claiming victimhood for ourselves, we get
to make whatever proclamation we want to about our supposed attackers,

and our celebrity doesn't hesitate on this score. She writes off not only her own attacker, but also all girls whom she perceives as causing pain. This is years later, by the way, which indicates that our celebrity hasn't gained any perspective on the situation. She presumes this girl is still the same, probably hanging out waiting for a chance to cut someone to the quick. This is hardly likely, but this is how victimhood and the Path of Least Resilience shapes our thinking.

When it comes to bullying on the Path of Least Resilience, the bad always outweighs the good, the problem always outweighs the solution, and the pain always outweighs the potential for understanding or growth. It's a road along which no one has take any responsibility for their feelings and they can rest easy in a singular interpretation of events, even if these interpretations aren't the complete story, or more importantly, even if these interpretations don't actually serve anyone. As our celebrity story illustrates, situations are *always* open to interpretation, although this fact has been lost to our current anti-bullying way of thinking. When you have a fixed mindset, there is only one interpretation available, and this interpretation has a name: the *truth*.

What isn't mentioned in all those celebrity testimonials is how the "bullying" positively contributed to who they are now. They don't acknowledge that perhaps their hardships created inner fortitude: that the experiences served as the proverbial wind. In our current climate, bullying is categorical bad and therefore it *shouldn't* happen, and we are not encouraged to see negative experiences as having any upside. Besides looking back and putting down the people who provided challenges—and feeling righteously superior—the anti-bullying movement doesn't allow for any positive side effect to the experience. If it did, then it would have to reconsider how damaging the bullying experiences really are. Who's to say getting teased about being short (or nerdy or red haired) wasn't the thing that propelled the above-mentioned celebrities into pursuing their craft, and therefore creating successful careers?[16]

---

16. I want to repeat that I understand these are mild cases of "bullying," however, this is where our expanded version of bullying has brought us. Mild or not, this is what is being paraded in front of us as bullying, and we are now expected to agree with the assessment of those who share their stories that these experiences qualify as victimization.

The lesson the anti-bullying movement is teaching our kids is that you should be able to go through childhood and adolescence *without* hardship, and that hardship is damaging. This runs completely counter to what we know about resilience. I wouldn't expect our celebrity to feel resilient or wise in the midst of her crying jag in the bathroom during high school, but now, at least 10 years later, it would serve her if she could see the experience for what it was—a bump in the road that could teach her something about herself. Unfortunately, the expanded definition of bullying doesn't encourage anyone to do this. Now that bullying is so broadly defined, our wounded celebrity, and everyone else, is encouraged instead to revisit old experiences and see nothing but damage and pain. Our definition of bullying, and our beliefs about the damage it causes, don't allow for a rethinking of the experience.

It is not enough to look back on these experiences and say, *I was bullied, and I went through hell—more hell than anyone else I know—but I'm so strong now because of it—bullies are evil and I am so much better than they are.* This is *not* resilience; this is clinging to victimhood in the guise of strength. Now consider the following statement and see if you can discern the differences in content and tone: *I went through a really hard time. It was tough, and I wish I hadn't gone through it, but I can see now that I learned something from it, even if it was painful. At least this experience taught me how to deal with things better. I guess we all go through hard times.*

That's resilience.

Victimhood and Resilience

Victimhood and resilience are antithetical. As long as we claim victimhood and feel like victims, we can't lay claim to resilience. In the same way we can't eat only sugar all day long and lay claim to health, we can't see only the bad and persecutory and expect to feel strong and robust—it just doesn't work that way. With the expanded definition of bullying, we are transforming people with normal painful experiences into victims by the millions, and in so doing opportunities to develop resilience are lost. Just listen to any bully "survivor" tell their tale and you'll understand what I'm saying.

There is a wonderful Buddhist parable that captures the essence of resilience. A mother loses her son; he dies. She is distraught, and she goes to the Buddha and asks him to bring her son back to her. The Buddha agrees, but under the condition that the woman brings to him a mustard seed from a home in which there hasn't been any suffering and loss. The woman is overjoyed so she readily agrees and proceeds to visit all the homes in her village. At each home she inquires about suffering and loss, and at each home she is told a different but equally painful tale of hardship. As she continues to search for her mustard seed, the woman hears about the wounds of all humanity. She is deeply humbled by this experience and, when she realizes that she will never find her mustard seed, she returns to the Buddha and asks to follow him.

This is not the lesson we are teaching our children when bullying is defined in such broad terms. The Buddha's lesson to the mother was that she was *not* a victim, and that by understanding the plight of others she could see her suffering for what it was: a painful but shared experience. This is a huge and profound life lesson—and it may take a lifetime to learn—but it's the lesson that leads to transformation, wisdom, and true resilience. Instead, the definition of bullying we have now sends kids the message that they can continue to see their suffering as victimization for as long as they want, maybe for a lifetime. In essence, this says to kids that it's okay for them to stay identified with their pain—consider those celebrities, for goodness sake; a decade later, and they're still thinking about their pain.

The Buddha's lesson provides context for everyone who is in pain, and it reminds us that we're not alone in our suffering. Strength doesn't come from identifying with suffering but rather from transforming in the face of it. Feeling like a victim at first, the woman in the parable gradually learned the true meaning of resilience, and it wasn't by simply overcoming her pain. The Buddha's lesson allowed her to transmute her suffering from lead into gold so that, in the end, she wasn't just a "survivor," she was something more. She was wise.

To be a bully "survivor" is to remain tied to the painful experience in a very immediate way—and to be defined by it—and this is not resilience (although it certainly passes for it lately; just read some of the "bully survivor" testimonials for proof). The suffering mother didn't just survive her pain, she understood it, accepted it, extracted meaning from it, and recognized it as an inevitable part of life. She didn't blog about it, that's for sure.

In the end, the Buddha didn't take away the mother's pain because he couldn't—and he understood this. But he gave her something tremendous nevertheless: the incomparable gift of wisdom.

Helicopter Parenting and the New Definition of Bullying

The new definition of bullying says much more about today's parenting than it does about childhood aggression. Kids haven't changed over the past few generations—they aren't more aggressive, or meaner, or more violent. Parents, on the other hand, are completely different animals than they were in past generations.

How are parents different today?

In a word, they hover, thus the term *helicopter parent*. Many parents believe they must be involved in every aspect of their children's lives, and that to do so constitutes good parenting; they try to oversee as much as they can. Helicopter parents are understandably anxious because they are trapped in a cycle of never-ending expectations of perfection. They try to monitor everything, which is impossible, yet this remains their goal, so they hover more, yet they still miss things, which makes them more anxious, and so on. They are vigilant and anxious and they feel frustrated and inadequate because they fall short of their expectations.

Before I continue, let me explain that I am not using the term helicopter parent in a derogatory light, despite the fact that it is generally used in this way. It is wonderfully descriptive term that captures they way many parents believe they are expected to behave, and as such it is a term that says more about our culture than it does about any particular parent. Helicopter parents are a product of the times. They evolved naturally, and the anti-bullying approach to childhood aggression and the attendant fear about children's safety evolved with them, and therefore the two are intimately connected.

Modern parents are faced with a daunting amount of information about parenting. There are literally thousands of parenting books on the market—*thousands*—which, even left unread, send parents the message that they better study up and pay attention if they want to do it right. The message includes the idea that they better want to do it right, and there's definitely a right way to do it, otherwise why would there be so many books written about parenting? This inundation of material would make anyone nervous about parenting, and helicopter parents are blanketed in this anxiety.

Modern parenting, and helicopter parenting—its most recent iteration—was invented in the second half of the 20th century. During this period, parents in America had more resources than ever before, fewer kids, a reduced reliance on their extended families (which means they didn't benefit as much from the collective wisdom of their own parents and grandparents when it came to parenting), and a burgeoning inclination for introspection that was previously unheard of. Mix all of these variables together, sprinkle a little Oprah on top, and out pops a parent who is self-reliant, self-aware, and prone to perfectionism and anxiety.

Our parents (and grandparents, depending on our age) had about one parenting book to refer to, *Dr. Spock's Baby and Childcare*, which was first published in 1946. Before then (and for long afterwards) parents weren't bombarded with advice on how to raise children. They just did it, and sometimes they did it badly. That sent many of us to therapy (also a relatively recent cultural invention), which made us want to do things differently with our own kids, which made us turn to Dr. Phil for advice, which made us buy every book that promised an easy fix for the incredibly difficult job of parenting. The helicopter parent emerged.

The parents I work with get much of their personal identity and self-esteem from being parents, and the media and all the parenting books on the market reinforce the idea that this is where they should get their sense of self-worth (*"parenting . . . the most important job in the world!"*). Most parents are highly attuned to what it means to be a "good" parent—even if that definition changes from expert to expert—and equally attuned to the ramifications of not being one; every parent I know takes their job as parent seriously, and they want to get it right.

Many conscientious parents I know adhere to the parenting philosophy of *more is more*. They want more information, more guidebooks, more blogs, more feedback, more interventions, more SAT prep courses, more tutoring, more psychological testing, more hand holding, more answers, more achievement, more *everything*. Okay, maybe they want less sugar for their kids, but that's about it; everything else is about *more*. This is what helicopter parenting is all about: hovering over children and assuming that as parents we must witness and orchestrate every detail of their lives so that the outcome is perfect.[17]

Which leads me back to our new definition of bullying, which is all about *more*: more things that can go wrong, more dangers to prevent, more damage to be done, more vigilance to be had. Parenting in the Age of Bullying is about doing more—more social engineering, more oversight, more worrying—and our definition of bullying provides fodder for this never-ending parental need. If parenting is a job, then bullying got added to the job description, and helicopter parents have taken it on with zeal.

Part of what makes this *more, more, more* philosophy possible is communication in the digital age. I spoke with a mother who had recently dropped off her daughter at college for her freshman year. Since the daughter's arrival at school, the mother and daughter had called, texted, or e-mailed each other every day—sometimes more than once a day, which provided the mother with lots of details about what her daughter was doing. Sometimes the details concerned frat parties, which caused the mother to worry; she knew from her own experience that frat parties could be a recipe for disaster for a young and naïve girl such as her daughter. As a result, when her daughter told her she was going to a frat party, the mother asked her to text her when she got home. If for some reason she didn't hear from her daughter, the mother became very anxious and called her early the next morning.

The daughter didn't seem to mind this level of involvement in her life—she had come to expect it, even rely on it. "Which is so ironic," the mother reported, "Because I would have killed my mother if she had been this involved in my life when I went away to college."

Ah, yes, the irony of helicopter parenting. When parents behave this way they are doing to their children what they would have hated being done to them, and they don't often appreciate this important point. It is normal to want independence and freedom from parents as we grow up. What helicopter parents want for their children is different, however.

---

17. For the sake of argument, I will assume that every parent reading this is a helicopter parent. Most of us are. It is now the cultural norm, and I don't use the term with any disrespect.

Helicopter parents want their children to stay connected to them, and digital technology has made this possible. Parents can track their children in a way parents couldn't in previous generations, and because they can, many of them do. The fact that we can track children's every move doesn't necessarily mean that we should, but tracking has become a natural part of a parent's job, so we want to track every aspect of our children's social lives, most especially when something goes wrong.

I want to emphasize the relationship between modern parenting and technology for a moment because our capacity for instantaneous and continuous connection has dramatically changed how parents can relate to children, and thus how they parent. Despite holding out the promise of reassuring us as parents, digital technology serves instead to increase parental anxiety more than anything else. If kids are out-of-range for too long, many parents start to worry, and out-of-range has a much different definition than it used to. It's not uncommon for parents to require their children to call them every step of the way whenever they go out, as though their cell phones are tracking devices.

"I just want to make sure you're safe," parents say to their kids. Or, "I need to be able to get in touch with you (or you need to be able to get in touch with me) if something happens." Whereas parents in the past may have wanted to have this kind of oversight of their kids, they simply couldn't, and therefore they didn't, so they had to accept that their children would have a certain degree of independence from them. No more. Now information and connection are what it's all about—good luck trying to buck that trend now. And in the absence of information and connection comes anxiety.

Anxiety is part-and-parcel of what it means to be a modern parent, and cell phones have increased this anxiety considerably. Now parents can hover more than ever, and they can peek into their children's lives in a way that wasn't possible in the past. Kids communicate with each other via text, Facebook, and e-mail, all of which parents can intrude upon. Privacy is a completely foreign concept in the age of connection, and it makes sense that we want to know everything that's going on with children, especially if we adhere to the *more is more* philosophy. Forget about freedom and independence; today's parents are interested in staying informed and connected.

I remember when cell phones first became popular, and kids began bringing them to school. I knew parenting had changed when I started getting calls from parents who were worried about what was happening with their children during the school day. "I just got a message from my daughter," one mother reported to me. "She had a fight with a friend. Can you check on her and see if she's okay?" Such an interchange would have been impossible until recently. Before children had regular use of cell phones, parents would never have known about a fight with a friend until the end of the school day, assuming kids chose to report it, and assuming kids even remembered it.

Parents may feel they have no choice but to be helicopter parents, and digital communication is a big part of it. How else are parents supposed to respond other than to hover when they get a call from a panicked child in the middle of the day? With constant digital access to parents, kids don't have to exercise any impulse control: they don't have to wait, calm themselves down, and try to solve problems on their own.

When children reach out to parents and they're *always* there—because they *can* be there—parents (and kids) assume that they *must* be there to attend to every expression of pain and distress because, well, that's what good parents do—they connect. They get involved. They pay attention. They respond. They solve problems, and there are many more problems to solve now because we are so connected to our children. But it is important to note that kids don't actually have more problems than they used to; it's just that we hear more about the problems than we used to.

Technology is wonderful, and there's nothing wrong with staying informed and connected, but there is a shadow side to the *more is more* parenting philosophy, and we can detect it in our approach to childhood aggression.[18] In the desire to stay connected and informed—and our culture has succeeded on these scores—parents are inclined to hover over

---

18. By *shadow side* I mean the side we don't readily see or acknowledge as being connected to a phenomenon. A shadow is the yang to the yin, or the back to its front. It's the downside, the drawbacks. For example, staying connected via technology is great but technology may dissuade us from actually connecting in person. Why go out of your way to see a friend when you can send a text? Is texting bad, per se? No, but it may have the undesired side effect of making us lose face-to-face connection with people. That's the shadow side.

their children's social lives in a way that gives us a unique perspective into their world. Parents know more about what's going on in the playground, who said what, what X posted online about Y, and with this comes the realization (or the memory) that kids can be really mean to one another, and with meanness comes pain.

More than anything else, helicopter parenting is about trying to prevent pain, despite the fact that, as a goal, preventing pain is undesirable in many cases. These hovering ways, and access to ample information, have given some parents what I call the Delusion of Omnipotence. These parents confuse the (perceived) omniscience that comes with hovering with the ability to do something with this information, and the notion that they should. When hovering parents hear that something's going wrong among kids, they believe they should do something about it.

This belief is diametrically opposed to most parenting approaches throughout history. It's fair to say we're in uncharted territory here because parents in the past simply didn't have the resources, desire, or wherewithal to oversee and intervene to the extent we do now. Modern parents have the resources, desire, and wherewithal in spades, plus they have the mandate that comes with the *more is more* philosophy, which is: what *can* be done *should* be done. Many parents also harbor the idea that comes with the Delusion of Omnipotence, which is that kids can't or shouldn't have to handle anything on their own. Helicopter parenting is rooted in the belief that kids have little capacity for resilience—that resilience isn't a natural thing that will develop over time—and that parents must provide the scaffolding for every experience kids have, good or bad. What is missing from helicopter parenting is trust and faith—in their own kids, in other kids, and in the process of growth and development.

Trust and faith used to be the foundations of parenting. I know of one mother whose approach to parenting exemplifies this. Betty had five children over the course of seven years. She was a stay-at-home mother (in the 1960s, she was called a housewife), and she and her family lived in the suburbs. In the morning, after the kids were dressed and fed, Betty gave each child a kiss and a pat on the head, shooed them into the back yard, told them to be good, and closed the door. And locked it. And kept it locked until lunch. In our current climate, Betty might get reported to Child Protective Services.

Betty's approach to parenting emphasized independence and resilience and parental sanity—Betty didn't want to entertain or oversee her kids all day; she had work to do. This sent Betty's kids the message that they could manage things on their own, within reason. Of course, Betty would have been available to them if her kids really needed her, but they would have had to climb over some hurdles to get her attention. Resilience begins for kids when they hear the click of that locking door. *I have to make this happen on my own.* By locking that door, Betty demonstrated to her kids that she had faith in them.[19]

Now, with the expanded definition of bullying, kids are being instructed that they should seek our help sooner rather than later, and that there are many things they will need help with, and that if they feel distressed at the hands of a peer this could be very problematic. By defining so many behaviors as bullying, anti-bullying initiatives have taught young people that the world is a dangerous place, which was the opposite message Betty gave her kids. Helicopter parents send the message that children shouldn't problem-solve on their own, they should seek help immediately when they feel distressed, and that their self-esteem could be crushed if they have to jump over some social hurdles. And, to repeat, the focus is on pain.

Pain, Pain, Go Away

The definition of bullying has ballooned for one primary reason: many of us want to prevent children from feeling pain.

No one wants to see children suffer; it can be excruciating. In fact, there's no bigger challenge for parents than to witness their children's suffering, and even worse, to feel helpless in the face of such suffering. A parent's instinct is to do everything in his or her power to protect a child from pain, and this is one of the driving forces behind our extremely broad definition of bullying. Parents have always understood the importance of keeping their children physically safe. Now they are attuned to keeping their children emotionally safe, and anti-bullying policies and legislation are an expression of this effort. In the desire to minimize our

---

19. Betty's kids are some of the most resilient adults I know. All five went to college and have interesting careers.

children's pain, the anti-bullying movement has made bullying an offense that includes almost any negative social behavior that can cause distress. We have confused being emotionally distressed with being unsafe, and in this confusion we have sought to protect children from some of the routine growing pains of childhood.

Some parents have internalized the belief that they should prevent their children's pain to the point where they feel guilty and responsible whenever their children feel anything negative. I once spent more than an hour on the phone with a mother who couldn't stand the fact that her daughter was sitting on the bench for most of her varsity soccer games. Her daughter came home angry and inconsolable after every game, and her mother didn't know what to do. She tried every trick in her parenting book: she told her daughter how great she was, how proud of her she was, how the coach was making a big mistake. Nothing worked, so she called me.

At first I thought this mother's complaints were about her daughter not getting her fair share of playing time, but they weren't. Instead, she felt paralyzed by her daughter's feelings of frustration and pain. This mother was under the impression that it was her job as a parent to take away her daughter's feelings of distress, and that the presence of her daughter's feelings was an indictment of her as a mother. This, then, made her feel terrible about herself, and she thought if she could only get the soccer coach to put her daughter on the field (or, more truthfully, if she could only get me to finagle this somehow), then everything would be fine. She was desperate to help her daughter (which to her meant solving all her daughter's problems for her) and in the process restore her own feelings of equilibrium as a parent. Suffice it to say, this approach was not a recipe for resilience, but it is the formula that many parents feel is their duty to follow.

Marion's case is another that highlights the tension between trying to protect children from pain and helping them build resilience in the face of that pain.

Marion's daughter, Abby, and Abby's "best friend," Tammy, were both eight years old. According to Marion, Tammy was domineering, insecure, and had no other friends besides Abby. Given these circumstances, Tammy wanted to keep Abby all to herself. When Abby tried to play with other kids at school, Tammy couldn't stand it. She "bullied" Abby back into their exclusive relationship and, when Abby strayed,

Tammy left Abby "bullying" voicemail messages. Tammy went so far as to enlist the help of other girls in her effort to keep Abby in line, and she had the other girls leave nasty messages for Abby as well. Tammy's campaign to keep Abby to herself extended to the Internet, where she "cyber-bullied" Abby. Tammy also stole passwords from other kids and used their e-mail accounts to bully Abby.

Marion was at a loss as to how to proceed. Abby was clearly miserable and didn't know how to handle the situation. She suffered migraines as a result of Tammy's behavior and had to stay home from school for a week. Naturally, Marion was extremely concerned; she was afraid for her daughter. Something had to be done. Marion didn't think the school could do much to manage the situation; Abby and Tammy's teacher required that the girls stay away from each other at recess, but this lasted for only a day. So, believing she had no other option for keeping Abby "safe," Marion decided to transfer Abby to another school. Even this didn't work. As Marion explained, Abby was a "follower" and, as a result, Tammy knew how to manipulate and bully her, and so the girls remained in touch, even after Abby enrolled at a different school.

Marion's concerns about her daughter were legitimate. Abby struggled to figure out the boundaries and to hold her ground with Tammy, and Tammy was clearly a powerful girl—she knew what buttons to push to get Abby to do her bidding. From Marion's perspective, Tammy had an almost magical ability to influence Abby's life and she exerted this power to Abby's detriment. In addition, and perhaps most importantly, Abby and Marion both felt awful about the situation. To Marion especially, the situation between the girls was so imbalanced and so unhealthy, and so obviously Tammy's fault, that something drastic had to be done to protect Abby. Something had to shift in the dynamic between the girls in order for Abby to regain a sense of equilibrium.

Most parents would share Marion's concerns under these circumstances, and Marion's response was in line with what parents have been lead to believe is the right thing to do when it comes to bullying: label what's going on and get children out of the line of fire as quickly as possible, before lasting damage is done. But did understanding the situation as bullying, and becoming as afraid as Marion did help her or Abby define their problems accurately and then deal with them effectively?

Let's consider Marion's situation first. Perhaps her biggest problem was watching her child suffer. Believing Abby was a "follower" made it even harder. Marion's fear and pain for Abby's wellbeing was magnified given that Abby, at least in Marion's eyes, had absolutely no control over her life. Marion saw bullying in the relationship between Abby and Tammy for a reason: she assumed Abby had no power and that Tammy had all of it. As long as Marion believed Abby was helpless, there was no way for her to see how the situation could be changed from within. Marion's view of the situation fit the definition of bullying perfectly, but it left her believing there was nothing Abby could do.

The other thing Marion believed was that an eight-year-old girl had the power to determine the course of her daughter's life. The fact that Marion believed that Tammy, who was the same age as Abby, could be so calculating and omnipotent closed her down to other interpretations of Tammy's behavior and, in turn, to other possible interventions for effective change. Lost to Marion in all of this was the obvious fact that Tammy wanted to be Abby's *friend*; Tammy was doing what she was doing because she liked Abby, not because she hated her. Tammy's behavior seemed like bullying from Marion's perspective—and by no means was it effective or nice behavior—but it was in the service of Tammy trying to get what she wanted, which was Abby's friendship. Tammy wasn't trying to destroy Abby's life; she was trying to be a part of it, however misguided her behavior was.

As the mother of a hurting child, it was not necessarily Marion's responsibility to explore the motivations of the child who she felt was mistreating her daughter, but doing so might have revealed to her other options for how to proceed. Removing a child from school is a very drastic measure, and Marion herself admitted that Tammy and Abby remained in contact after Abby left school. This leads me to another aspect of this situation that Marion overlooked: Abby was getting something out of this relationship, however much it pained her.

I can't presume to say what Abby was getting from Tammy, but she was getting something. If Abby wanted to break off contact with Tammy, then changing schools would have achieved this goal pretty effectively (that, and not answering phone calls or e-mails).[20] But Abby stayed connected to Tammy after the fact, which underscores the fact that what happened between the girls was not solely Tammy's responsibility. Had Marion considered this as a possibility before removing Abby from school, she might have been able to consider other, less drastic, courses of action, such as helping Abby advocate for herself, and to explore what, if anything, she got out of her relationship with Tammy.

Marion did what she thought she had to do to keep Abby safe, but this wasn't enough and it wasn't effective. And safe from what—her feelings? Amidst all of our concerns about bullying, it's almost anathema to declare that safety isn't enough, but it isn't. Parents must consider both safety *and* resilience when they consider how to proceed, but the new definition of bullying, because it is so broad and vague, makes this a much more difficult calculation to make than ever before. Almost any repeated negative behavior, if the recipient feels harmed, constitutes bullying, and therefore much of what our children experience at the hands of their peers is considered dangerous.

Marion believed that a) her daughter was being bullied, and b) bullying is really harmful, and therefore she cast aside the opportunity for Abby to develop resilience. And Marion isn't alone. Once a situation is labeled as bullying, the issue of resilience no longer matters, and this is problematic. We are simply paralyzed by fear about bullying, as Marion was, but we should be equally scared about what our kids are missing in terms of developing resilience.

Abby's situation bears this out. Regardless of how well intended Marion's actions were, they taught Abby an object lesson in the lack of resilience. Most significantly, Marion saw Abby as a follower (victim), and as we saw in Chapter 1, labels create a fixed view of the world for everyone involved in the situation. Even if Marion never told Abby she thought she was a follower, her actions demonstrated it. By removing Abby from school, Marion communicated to her that she wasn't strong enough to deal with the situation, and that the situation as it stood would never change.

The acceptance of change, growth, and development is a cornerstone

---

20. This leads me to wonder why an eight-year-old child has an e-mail account or regular access to voicemail.

of resilient thinking. Everything changes; nothing stays the same, but this truth was lost on Marion.

Remember, Tammy and Abby were eight years old. *Every* child changes, *every single one of them*, as do their circumstances. They learn new skills, meet new people, make new friends, get new teachers, go on summer vacation and spend time away from their classmates, and throughout all of this their brains continue to mature (more on this in Chapter 3). Every new variable creates a new world for them. Abby was going to change, Tammy was going to change, and therefore their relationship was going to change, possibly not without guidance from adults, but things were going to change. Change was inevitable.

Marion made sure Abby didn't learn any of this from her dilemma with Tammy, however. Instead, when Marion pulled her out of school, Abby learned:

1. My mother doesn't have faith that I will change and can develop new skills to take care of myself.

2. I am a follower and this situation happened because I have no control over myself or what happens to me.

3. Other people are more powerful than I am.

4. Other people control and determine the course of my life.

5. When a situation gets tough, the best plan is to bail out—to let the other person get the better of you.

6. My pain is unbearable, impossible to deal with, and harmful.

7. My mother can't tolerate my pain.

This final point is perhaps the most crucial one. Marion was overwhelmed by Abby's pain, and she feared it would do Abby great harm. Believing her daughter to be a victim of bullying, Marion responded the way many parents do, which is to assume that her daughter's pain was an indication of lasting and permanent damage. There's no such thing as good bullying, so once parents accept that their children have been bullied (which is very easy to do, given the broad definition), they have a tendency to interpret their children's emotions as dangerous, damaging, and something to halt immediately. This is what Marion did.

Rather than dealing with the problem, however, Marion's actions added to it. Abby continued to feel helpless and victimized, in part because her mother refused to see her in any other light. Marion's actions ensured that Abby never had the chance to consider her own behavior and to learn from it or to develop the skills she needed to be able to deal with the next problematic situation coming down the pike, and no doubt it was coming. As a "follower," Abby was sure to face another Tammy in the future, and, unfortunately for her, she hadn't learned enough from her situation with the first Tammy to adequately prepare her for the next one.

Ironically, rather than helping Abby develop some skills to prevent her from being vulnerable to similar situations in the future, Marion's beliefs and actions reinforced in Abby the very traits that got her into trouble in the first place. What Marion didn't consider was that Abby's pain, while significant, was a symptom of something more than just her situation with Tammy. Yes, Abby's pain was connected to Tammy's behavior, but it wasn't just about that. Abby's pain was as much about Abby as it was about Tammy, and these messages never got heard in Marion's desire to remove the pain.

There was actually one very valuable takeaway from this scenario available to both Marion and Abby, had they known about and chosen to pay attention to it, and that was the old Buddhist saying, *wherever you go, there you are.* Changing schools may have altered the backdrop of the situation, but it didn't change Abby (or Marion), and Abby's continued connection with Tammy proved it. Sadly for Abby, though, Marion continued to see the girls' relationship as both wholly negative and wholly Tammy's fault, which limited Abby's ability to develop resilience from the situation.

Marion can't be faulted for her actions. She was the mother of a suffering child. From this standpoint (and this standpoint only), she acted with the best of intentions when she removed Abby from school. In fact, what Marion did is becoming more common. Given our broad definition of bullying and our cultural hysteria about it, Marion was doing what she thought best: she attempted to stop the situation, rather than working to change it.

The broad definition of bullying has rendered much of childhood pain threatening and dangerous, so parents like Marion are left with no other options but to respond with drastic measures. There *were* other responses available to Marion, if only she had been able to think about the situation differently, but she couldn't, not through the haze that has enveloped our culture due to our belief that childhood aggression is dangerous and that bullying is everywhere.

Della's situation was similar to Abby's in many ways, although Della was a little older (about eleven) when she struggled with a particular friend, Caroline. I met Della when she was an adult, long after she made it through the gauntlet of childhood and once she had some perspective about what had happened to her. Della described feeling completely overwhelmed by the negative interactions she had with Caroline during middle school. Caroline taunted Della, spread rumors about her, and did everything in her power to intimidate and control her. Caroline eventually succeeded in turning many of Della's friends against her.

Della had no idea what to do at the time and she did not tell her parents or teachers about it. This was before situations like Della's were considered bullying, and before children routinely sought help from adults to deal with their social situations. It never crossed Della's mind to involve her parents or the school—it just wasn't an option. Della knew she was on her own and she could see no immediate solution to the situation. She tried to persuade Caroline to like her and she altered her behavior hoping the other girls would accept her again. Nothing worked, and so Della withdrew into herself and spent hours contemplating her fate and questioning the meaning and limits of friendship.

Della's situation changed slowly. She gradually reached out to some other classmates, girls she had never really connected with before, and started forming new friendships. At the beginning of 7th grade, Caroline was assigned a different homeroom, so Della didn't have to see her as much anymore, although Caroline continued to shun her when their paths crossed. Over time, Della realized that the world hadn't come to an end as a result of what had happened. She even realized that her life was better now that some of her former friends were no longer in the picture. The whole situation gave her the opportunity to consider things such as loyalty, trust, and honesty, and her ability to weather a pretty nasty storm.

As an adult, Della was clear that her situation with Caroline had been hard and even traumatic—time hadn't lessened her memories of acute pain. Caroline's behavior had turned Della's social world upside down, but it also made Della think. Della discovered that she was strong, and that her friendship was worth something. Her new friends were very different than Caroline, and they made her see her worth. Della was quick to admit that none of her adult wisdom would have soothed her at the time. As a kid, she felt adrift and lost but, in retrospect, she realized how much she learned from the situation. In retrospect, Della was glad for the pain because she knew it had caused her to grow, and she doubts she would have come through childhood with the degree of confidence she had in herself without it.

Della is now a middle school teacher and she often wonders whether her own students are being prevented from learning the lessons she learned. Della didn't have the benefit of the kinds of intervention we make with kids, but she got something more, and she wonders whether our new definition of bullying is providing short-term solutions for much bigger issues. The struggle Della went through made her who she is; it didn't detract from her growth, but this is how we currently think. Many adults are quick to say how much better their lives would be if they hadn't been bullied as kids, but is this true? If we consider only pain, then perhaps yes, but if we factor in resilience, as Della does, then the answer isn't as simple.

Abby and Della were in similar social boats, but while Abby's situation is a case study of victimhood, Della's is a case study in resilience.

Interviewing for Pain

Ted, age 10, had lots of trouble with his classmate Jack. Ted was often the brunt of Jack's taunts and meanness, and Brad, Ted's father, was extremely concerned about both Jack's behavior and Ted's reaction to it. Brad felt it was his duty as a parent to make sure his son felt safe and protected at all times and, to this end, Brad believed he needed to monitor Ted's situation closely, which he did by constantly asking Ted questions about it.

When Brad dropped off Ted at school in the morning, his last words to his son were, *Be careful—don't let Jack bully you!* When he picked him at the end of the school day, Brad asked, *How was Jack today? Did he bully you again?* Before Ted even had the chance to fasten his seatbelt, Brad peppered him with the questions, asking about Jack's specific behavior and Ted's pain in response to it. *Are you okay? Did you get hurt? Do you feel threatened?*

Brad went through this routine every day, not just when Ted indicated something was wrong. If Ted reported that things were fine with Jack, Brad was cautious about dropping the subject too soon. He worried he might miss something, and that maybe Ted would feel unsupported. Brad wanted Ted to know that Brad "had his back," and that he could tell Brad everything. When Ted said something positive about Jack, Brad couldn't accept it. *Well, he might have been friendly today, but don't trust that kid. He's a bully.*

In his desire to oversee and manage Ted's situation, Brad did something many parents do: he interviewed for pain. By this I mean he asked loaded questions, which required Ted to focus on the negative aspects of any encounter he had with Jack. Each of Brad's questions framed Ted's situation in such a way that there was nothing but pain to report; anything less than struggle and angst didn't meet Brad's threshold of interest. This, in turn, gave Ted the message that the only things Brad cared about were Jack's bullying behaviors and Ted's reactions to them, which of course wasn't the case. Brad cared most about Ted's well-being, and he thought his questions were the best way to support his son and to ferret out any problems.

As a result, Ted started and ended each school day thinking that pain and victimhood were par for the course. Ted began to anticipate his father's questions and spent much of the school day cataloguing his interactions with Jack, knowing his dad wouldn't take him off the hook until he had supplied the appropriate responses. Every morning Ted steeled himself against the pain that was certain to come, and every afternoon he dutifully reported every misstep that Jack took and every feeling he had in response. And each day he felt a little more dread and a little less in control of his life.

Much to Brad's surprise and dismay, things between Ted and Jack didn't improve. In fact, Ted started to wither under Brad's scrutiny, although he was too young to understand why. A teenager might have told his father to back off or given him the silent treatment, but Ted was compliant, confusing Brad to no end about why the situation wasn't improving. Brad figured he was bolstering Ted's self-esteem by talking openly about Jack the Bully, and he assumed his constant reminders to Ted about staying vigilant would solve the problem. They didn't; they just reminded Ted that his feelings of pain were the most important thing to keep track of, more so than any of his many accomplishments.

As Brad continued to monitor the situation, he contemplated taking Ted out of school, as Marion had done with Abby. Luckily for Ted, though, he was spared the upheaval. Before making a decision, Brad shared his concerns with one of the school administrators, a woman who knew Ted and his situation well. When Brad explained what was happening, the administrator immediately picked up on Brad's penchant for interviewing for pain. At first Brad was confused—wasn't he doing the right thing by asking Ted lots of questions and expressing his concern? The administrator pointed out that whereas Brad's impulse to protect his son was a good one, his technique for doing so made Ted feel less supported and less in control of his situation, not more.

Brad's focus on his son's pain kept it alive for Ted, and it made him think not only that the discomfort he sometimes felt was never going to change but that it was never *supposed* to change. When Brad interviewed for pain, Ted kept having it, in part because he came to think of pain as natural and expected. Brad admitted that one of the reasons he was so focused on Ted's pain was because Brad had felt a lot of pain as a kid: he had a very hard time when he was Ted's age and he was determined to protect Ted from going through the same things he did.

Brad was determined to turn the situation around and so he stopped his incessant questioning. He let Ted take the lead when the subject of Jack came up, and he focused more on helping Ted solve problems than on identifying them. Slowly but surely Brad calmed down, and so did Ted. Over time, Brad was able to see how much his own anxiety had contributed to Ted's feelings of insecurity and fear around Jack, and once Brad's feelings and behavior changed—no more pestering questions—Ted was able to focus on other things. None of this happened immediately, and sometimes Brad slipped and interrogated Ted about Jack, but gradually things shifted. Ted remained at school, where many things went well for him, and by the following year his entire social world had been transformed. Jack became a non-entity in Ted's life and Ted started to feel confident. Gone was the tentative, hesitant boy and in his place emerged a self-possessed young man. Without the threat of pain hanging over him, Ted was free to explore who he really was, and Brad couldn't have been more proud.

Interviewing for pain is one of the most effective ways of creating scared and tentative children. Imagine if every day Brad had asked Ted about his stomachache. *How does your stomach feel this morning? Make sure you don't get a stomachache at school today! Did lunch make you nauseous? Did you throw up again?* If I weren't confident that such an experiment would work (and therefore hurt kids), I would challenge parents to ask their kids about their stomachaches every day, morning and night, for a week. I can guarantee a few things would happen.

First, many kids would develop stomachaches. Second, some kids would withdraw and tell their parents to leave them alone. Finally, every child would feel a host of negative emotions, from irritation, to fear, to anger, to exasperation, to resentment, and they might even start throwing up. None of them would feel good, not one. We would never think of asking kids incessantly about their stomachaches, and yet we think this technique will help when it comes to their emotional health. It doesn't.

From my standpoint, interviewing for pain has become much more common now that the definition of bullying has expanded. Many parents are running scared and they think interviewing for pain is the way to protect their kids. Paradoxically, this technique doesn't open kids up. It shuts them down. It also makes the prospect of feeling pain inevitable for kids, and it sets up a dynamic whereby in order to be compliant and dutiful, children must feel distress. Interviewing for pain draws attention to problems that aren't necessarily there and makes the problems that are there even worse.

Good and conscientious parents interview for pain all the time because they've been warned that danger is everywhere. Childhood is filled with lots of things—joy, growth, mastery of skills, challenges—but the thing parents are focused on now is danger, and interviewing for pain is a well intended but ineffective way to prevent and deal with danger.

The Focus on Feelings, and Feelings as Facts

What seems of paramount importance when it comes to bullying is the victim's response to what's happening, sometimes even more than whatever behavior is (supposedly) causing the feelings. When a behavior such as *persistent unfriendliness* reaches the threshold of bullying, as it does in some anti-bullying policies, this point is clear. Admittedly, it feels bad to be on the receiving end of persistent unfriendliness, but does this justify defining this behavior as bullying? According to many policies it does, and this sends a powerful and dangerous message to children.

Teaching children that something like repeated unfriendliness—or many of the other non-physical behaviors—is bullying is instructing them that their *feelings* are what's most important when it comes to determining the nature of a negative social interaction, and that their *feelings are facts*. Of course, feelings, especially for children, are often the most salient piece of information they have about what happening to them. But are they everything? And are they enough when it comes to making the charge of bullying? For many, the answer is yes.

One day I was consulted by another school counselor who had spoken with the mother of an 8-year-old boy who was having problems with his peer group. During recess, this boy wanted to be included with a group of boys who spent their time roughhousing, playing dodge ball, and running circles around each other. These boys were energetic and playful and thick-skinned, and they weren't interested in adapting their activities to accommodate this other boy who was naturally more gentle and sensitive. He was allowed to play with them only if he agreed to their rules. Unfortunately, he didn't know how to join them on their terms, and so he was excluded. And, sadly for him, the harder he tried to be included, the worse he felt when he couldn't be like the other boys.

Over time, this started to wear on the boy and he occasionally asked his teacher if he could stay inside at recess or he sat alone on the playground feeling dejected. His mother saw how much he was suffering. She tried everything she could to help her son join in with his peers. She coached him on how to approach the boys, gave him tips about what to say, and told him how to stand up for himself in the face of rejection. Nothing seemed to work. After no success and repeated rebuffs and rejections—some of which were pretty harsh—her son felt terrible about himself. He even told his mother that he didn't enjoy school anymore because of all the rejection. Some days he cried as he left home in the morning, overwhelmed with sadness about the rejection that was sure to come.

Naturally, his mother was distressed by all of this. She couldn't stand to see her son suffer in this way; he was such a nice kid, and he tried so hard. All he wanted was to be included; the repeated rejection was taking a toll on his ability to concentrate at school and, as a result, on his ability to make the most of his education. Given his diminished capacity to function happily at school, his mother felt that her son's patience and good will had been exhausted, his classmates had crossed the line, and their behavior was unacceptable. It was one thing to exclude her son occasionally but quite another to do so on a daily basis. This had to stop, and thus she contacted the school in order to get help with the bullying.

On the face of it, all of the criteria for bullying were met: persistent social exclusion (at least according to both mother and son); persistent unfriendliness; the dominance of one group of kids over one child; and the wounded feelings of the victim. Given all of this, the mother pressed the school to respond. But what was it responding to, once the boy's feelings of loneliness and isolation were taken out of the equation?

This is a pretty common scenario in my experience, where we treat feelings as facts rather than as fluid and ever-changing variables that are part of a bigger picture. Because this boy *felt* bullied, he *was* bullied, and his feelings became fact—even though the "bullies" in question would have allowed him to play if he had played by their rules. When children's feelings are allowed to become fact, this doesn't leave them with any problem-solving tools. Children should be taught to recruit their intellects to deal with difficult situations. If we leave them hanging with just their feelings, then we don't help them develop resilience.

Sticks and Stones

When I was a kid, we had a standard response to our peers' verbal assaults and meanness: *sticks and stones may break my bones but words will never hurt me.* All the kids used this phrase, and in my neighborhood we added a little melody, so it became sort of a song. This retort served as a shield against what we didn't want to hear, and it was our way of letting others know that they couldn't harm us with words. I heard this phrase repeatedly during childhood: on the playground, on the street, in the school hallways—all the places kids interacted with one another. It was a way to set a boundary, to tell someone to back off, and to reestablish equilibrium.

Did this method magically solve all our problems? Hardly. Did it stop the taunts from coming? Not necessarily. Did it mend all of our wounds? Nope. Did it make us feel better? Well, sort of, and here's why.

This powerful little phrase communicated a lot to us as children. It let us know that we had (or could have) control of our feelings, and that we were strong inside, regardless of what other people said about us. It was the cornerstone of a conceptual framework that gave us a strategy for self-protection in the moment of confrontation, and it provided some measure of reassurance and strength. It didn't prevent us from feeling our feelings or from feeling hurt—and sometimes feeling really hurt—but it gave us the message that we could handle what other people said, and that the insult and any pain we felt as a result wouldn't destroy us. *Sticks and stones* acted like a talisman; it was a verbal amulet that we carried in our emotional toolbox.

This phrase sent us the message that we could handle whatever was out there, regardless of what we felt like in the moment, which, again, could be really bad. It gave us a sense of reassurance and confidence, even if we didn't have confidence ourselves, and it gave us permission to not retreat in the face of another person's opinion. The phrase also helped us make a distinction between physical and psychological wounds. That's what really gave us power—as long as we weren't being hurt physically, this phrase taught us that we could take it. It also brought a measure of perspective to the situation. When we used this retort it meant that we weren't getting hurt physically, and that we should understand that pain as being relative.

Another saying we used was *I know you are, but what am I?* We used this interchangeably with *sticks and stones*, but it had a little more punch. Whereas *sticks and stones* served as a deflection ("You can't hurt me"), *I know you are, but what am I?* gave it back to the aggressor in kind. It was a counter taunt, not just a retort. If someone called you stupid, for instance, saying *I know you are, but what am I?* made sure you got in the last word, and it put the onus back on the other person to come up with something that could *really* hurt. You could repeat this phrase endlessly, and often interchanges between kids came to a halt due to sheer annoyance and boredom.

More than anything else, the phrases *sticks and stones* and *I know you are, but what am I?* were methods of disengagement. They aren't quite as disengaging as walking away or completely ignoring a situation, but they are almost as effective at getting the energy of an attack to lose its momentum. This doesn't mean these phrases prevented us from being attacked or hurt; they didn't. And as I said, they also didn't protect us from *feeling* attacked or hurt. But every time we used them, and every time they were used against us, they reminded us that our opinion of ourselves was more important than anyone else's and that we weren't victims.

How things have changed.

One of the first indications I had that things were shifting in our cultural approach to childhood aggression was when, in the mid-2000s, I heard about a school that draped a banner across its threshold that read *sticks and stones can break my bones and words can* really *hurt me*. My first response was confusion, in part because I didn't get it—the saying just didn't make sense anymore as a retort. Was this what kids were now supposed to sing to their aggressors? Was this the new talisman against pain? Of course not. Now it was an object lesson in victimhood. I realized in that moment that by replacing the word *never* with the word *really*, our entire approach to childhood aggression had changed.

Sticks and stones can break my bones and words can really *hurt me* now communicates something entirely different to kids. The message of the first version is, in effect, "You don't have any power over me—your words are meaningless and I am in control of how I feel about and see myself." The message of the second is, "You have a lot of power over me—your words can determine whether or not I feel good about myself."

So, not only have the words and meaning of the phrase changed but so has the purpose. The original saying was about *rejecting* the insult. The revised version is about *accepting* it.

It's not that the new, revised phrase is untrue—of course other people can hurt our feelings, but the objective of the first phrase is to fight our inclination to take on and identify with this pain, and to let the aggressor know as much. It communicates to the aggressor that we are strong, and that we can take whatever they dish out. With the new, modified phrase, kids are instructed to accept the pain, and to let the aggressor know that they've accepted it. You don't have to be a psychologist to recognize the implications of this shift. If I say something to get under your skin and you indicate that I have not succeeded (*sticks and stones* version one), then I eventually stop. If I say something to get under your skin and you indicate that I have succeeded (version two), then I keep going. This is especially true if the aggressor's goal is to hurt you. Version two is the payoff they're waiting for; version one is not.

This shift from *words can never hurt* to *words can really hurt* is effectively complete. I was in a middle school social studies classroom recently where students had been instructed to make posters illustrating important concepts. My eye was drawn to a poster that read Words Can Hurt. Underneath was a cartoon of one person's words cascading out of his mouth and showering another person on the ground. Alongside the cartoon, students had written what Words Can Hurt meant to them:

- Making fun of someone
- Verbal abuse
- Foul language
- Negative criticism
- Words can hurt more than actions because even though it doesn't hurt you physically, it will hurt you mentally.

It *will* hurt you mentally, and now, at least according to these middle school students the mental is even more harmful than the physical. The takeaway for these students is that you should have an even greater response to mental distress than to physical pain, and that something like foul language could be the culprit. Foul language *will* hurt you mentally? I have no doubt that foul language might be offensive, but hurtful? When kids are educated to believe that foul language will hurt (or when they educate each other, as was the case with this school poster), they get positioned for a lifetime of frustration and distress, distress they will not be able to manage effectively because they see the cause and resolution of that pain as coming from without.

Eleanor Roosevelt once said, "No one can make you feel inferior without your consent."[21] When I first heard this statement, perhaps when I was

---

21. It is unclear when Mrs. Roosevelt spoke these words, although by 1940 the quote appeared in *Reader's Digest*. When I try to explain this sentiment to younger children, I sometimes paraphrase the statement thus: no one can make

in my mid teens, I was transfixed. It was a very sophisticated reworking of *sticks and stones*—the adult version, shall we say—and it simply blew me away. Up until that point, and despite the *sticks and stones* mantra, I had never really considered the part each of us plays in the creation of our own psychological wounds. I believed that other people did mean things to you, and you got hurt as a result—end of story. But Eleanor Roosevelt's declaration rejected this worldview and held out the promise of a capacity for inner strength and fortitude I never thought possible, at least not for me. At the time I remember thinking, *You mean, I can actually do something about this? I have the power to choose? I have control over this?*

Our culture, in the heat of its anti-bullying fever, has rejected Eleanor Roosevelt's wisdom. When there's a poster on a classroom wall that declares *words will hurt you mentally*, then we've effectively swung to the other end of the pendulum, and this is where our broad definition of bullying has landed us. In an effort to keep children (presumably) safe, we have taken all responsibility for their emotional reactions off their plates, and in the process they are being denied important opportunities for self-reflection and resilience.

---

you feel bad without your permission. quoteinvestigator.com/2012/04/30/no-one-inferior/.

CHAPTER 3

ZERO TOLERANCE SETS
KIDS UP TO FAIL

Good judgment comes from experience,
experience comes from bad judgment.
-Mark Twain

Zero Tolerance

Zero Tolerance is a stand many schools, parents, legislative bodies, and anti-bullying advocates support as a way to combat childhood aggression. Zero Tolerance means no tolerance for behaviors that meet our current definition of bullying. The following are some statements that represent the stand of Zero Tolerance advocates:

Bullying needs to be a community issue and we must have a zero tolerance policy. We have to create a standard in the community that will have a domino effect where kids know that if they bully, there will be consequences.[1]

Bullying is not going to go away if we ignore it and pretend it is not an issue. It needs to be faced head-on. Bullies need to be dealt with and not allowed to run the schools. We adults have to take a stand that bullying

---

1. Dr. Robi Ludwig, psychotherapist based in New York City, October 10, 2010. www.huffingtonpost.com/wendy-sachs/new-poll-finds-bullying-i_b_768958.html

will no longer be tolerated in our schools, our ballparks, our communities, etc.[2]

The public—adult and kids alike—needs to view bullying as something that brands you with a modern-day scarlet letter . . . There needs to be a palpable stigma attached [to being a bully] . . . Our zero tolerance policies are a good start.[3]

It's time we not only put a stop to bullying, but more, that we adopt a zero-tolerance policy on bullying of all kinds. Read that again: zero-tolerance. Zero, as in none, nada, zip. No bullying now and in perpetuity.[4]

As you can see, Zero Tolerance advocates are passionate about putting an end to bullying, and many are clearly frustrated that bullying continues to persist in the face of our united opposition to it. No one wants children to feel pain or to suffer. No one wants children to hurt one another. Everyone wants schools to be safe and harmonious environments. Given that we all agree on these things, the Zero Tolerance approach to bullying makes sense, at least on the face of it. It's simple, straightforward, and clear cut. *Just say no to bullying!*

Unfortunately, childhood aggression isn't as simple, straightforward, or as clearcut as anti-bullying advocates would like it to be. Nevertheless, many embrace Zero Tolerance because it satisfies a desire to take action— to *do* something—and stamping out the problem is an understandable desire given the way our culture currently thinks about childhood aggression.

In many ways, we arrived at Zero Tolerance naturally. As I explained in Chapter 1, Bully Language creates a fixed mindset about childhood aggression, and this conceptual framework causes us to feel both persecuted and righteous. In Chapter 2, I examined how the broad definition of bullying ensures that we see the problem everywhere, and this

---

2. Elena Wright, September 27, 2011, *North Jefferson News* online, www.njeffersonnews.com/features/x780410375/Schools-parents-should-place-zero-tolerance-on-bullying.

3. Todd Patikin, p. 7, *Westside Observer,* November 2011.

4. Dr. Susan Corso, *Huffington Post,* October 26, 2010, www.huffington-post.com/dr-susan-corso/gay-bullying_b_765618.html.

leaves many of us feeling helpless and overwhelmed. As a result, when it comes to childhood aggression, many feel persecuted, righteous, helpless, and overwhelmed. It's no wonder, then, that Zero Tolerance is a popular response. *Just say no* makes sense in this cultural atmosphere. When the problem is crafted in absolute terms where there is a clear enemy (the bully) and when only one side of the story gets told and problematic situations are devoid of context, then anti-bullying advocates can fairly proclaim: *Zero, as in none, nada, zip. No bullying now and in perpetuity.*[5]

Despite the logic, Zero Tolerance is in fact a fixed mindset solution to a fixed mindset problem. Zero Tolerance may be the next step down the path of the current thinking about childhood aggression, but it's leading us in the wrong direction. The truth is that childhood aggression isn't so clear cut, children are not the enemy, and all sides of the story must be taken into consideration when it comes to educating and guiding children. In the end, rather than keeping kids safe, Zero Tolerance sets them up to fail because it presumes they can control themselves at all times, that they should always behave in certain ways (and never in others), and that they should never make specific mistakes (and never more than once). If and when children do transgress, Zero Tolerance holds out the promise of punishment and scarlet letter labeling (which is a serious punishment in and of itself). As a result, it teaches kids about one of the central planks of the fixed mindset platform: that your mistakes define you.

Furthermore, Zero Tolerance falls short as a solution to the problems kids have with each other because it doesn't take into consideration the reality of childhood development and the process by which children must learn to manage their aggression.

In its uncompromising way, Zero Tolerance doesn't acknowledge that kids are different at every stage of their growth, and that what we can expect of a six-year-old is vastly different than what we can expect of a teenager. Having the same policies for both, and defining misbehavior in the same way for both, is to miss the essence of development entirely. Children of every age deserve to be guided by policies and procedures that focus on learning and growth, not solely on prohibitions and

---

5. Dr. Susan Corso, *Huffington Post,* October 26, 2010, www.huffington-post.com/dr-susan-corso/gay-bullying_b_765618.html.

consequences, although these elements are important too. To this end, Zero Tolerance policies do not reflect an understanding of learning or development, and in this way they create standards for children that are off-base at best and harmful at worst.

Throughout this chapter, I will examine the various responses our culture currently has to childhood aggression in the forms of policies and procedures, particularly Zero Tolerance. I will also review specific aspects of childhood development, in particular the middle-school years—during which many of the behaviors that are defined as bullying seem to flourish—and explore how well our current policies match the needs of children at these various stages of development.

History of Zero Tolerance

The term Zero Tolerance was in use long before bullying came into our cultural awareness. It was originally adopted in the early 1980s as part of the rhetoric against drug use (along with Nancy Reagan's *Just Say No* anti-drug campaign) but gained traction in 1994 when President Clinton signed the Gun-Free Schools Act. Students who were caught in violation of the Gun-Free Schools Act faced an automatic expulsion from school for one year, plus referral to either the criminal or juvenile justice systems—thus, Zero Tolerance.

Since then Zero Tolerance has become a stance that many educators, schools, and parents have adopted to combat a wide variety of childhood misbehaviors. From drugs to guns to "fighting . . . and swearing," many have turned to Zero Tolerance as the best way to combat the many problems facing today's youth.[6] It makes sense, then, that bullying would get added to this list. If Zero Tolerance was an appropriate method to use against other ills, then why not use it for bullying? If we look a little deeper, we see that many aspects of childhood aggression, as they are expressed in so-called bullying behaviors, are fundamentally different than other issues we've fought with Zero Tolerance, and that the challenges we face aren't well suited to a Zero Tolerance approach.

---

6. Safe and Responsive Schools Project at the Indiana Education Policy Center, www.indiana.edu/~safeschl/zero.html.

For example, there is never any reason for a child to have a gun at school. Never, under any circumstances, does having a gun at school serve children, and furthermore, marksmanship isn't part of the curriculum (and if it is, then certainly children aren't allowed to walk around the hallways with guns, store them in their lockers, or use them to threaten or injure other people). Even the most strident gun supporters would agree that children having guns at school is a bad idea. The Zero Tolerance approach is easy to support on this score.

Another no-brainer is the possession, selling, and use of illegal and illicit drugs by children, especially at school. We can easily agree on Zero Tolerance for this issue as well. Using illicit drugs isn't part of the curriculum, having drugs around doesn't further or support a child's education or development, and drugs don't contribute to the smooth functioning of the school community. They're unhealthy and dangerous, not to mention illegal, so Zero Tolerance is a perfectly understandable position to take when it comes to drugs—we're just not going to put up with them, end of story.

As you can see, the Zero Tolerance approach isn't problematic in and of itself, but it's the wrong tactic to address our current dilemma because childhood aggression isn't an either-or proposition. Solutions must match problems in order to be effective, and the Zero Tolerance solution simply isn't a good match for many of the problems that arise from childhood aggression. A Zero Tolerance position makes sense when it comes to guns in schools because guns have no inherent place in schools, and it's a choice to possess them: They aren't surgically attached to our arms. The same holds true for illegal drugs. No one has to use them; they aren't part of who we are, nor are they necessary, especially in the pursuit of an education. Guns and drugs come from the outside, they play no beneficial role or purpose in children's lives, and everyone can happily do without them in schools. Childhood aggression, on the other hand, is a completely different issue.

For starters, aggression is something all kids must contend with—their own, as well as their classmates'—and they can't just leave it at home. Aggression is as much a part of them as intelligence, or athleticism, or artistic sensibility. A big part of childhood development involves understanding and managing impulses, aggression included. So, unlike guns or drugs, dealing with aggression is very much a part of the curriculum in childhood. Once we accept this fact we must then consider dealing with aggression as a critical part of social emotional development in childhood.

While it is certainly true that there must be rules and standards of behavior for children, they can't just be told not to bring an essential part of themselves to school. A gun, sure, leave it at home, and while you're at it, leave the illegal drugs at home as well. But aggression? Children can't do it, and the Zero Tolerance approach doesn't take this into consideration. When it comes to managing aggressive impulses, every child will fail at some point because every child gets frustrated and angry and makes mistakes along the way—*every* one of them, not just the "bad" kids. With this in mind, it's important to recognize that we are destined for a future of frustration and anger if we insist on Zero Tolerance, especially now that so many childhood mistakes have been repackaged as bullying.

Kids get set up to fail when they are told that, under no circumstances, should they make mistakes that involve something they must wrestle with a lot of the time (their tempers, for instance, or their capacity to include or be nice to others). This is markedly different than telling them that they should never, under any circumstances, bring guns or drugs to school. Kids aren't set up to fail with these prohibitions because children don't need to do these things, and they aren't being tempted. If guns were handed out at school and kids were told not to touch them, or if illegal drugs were distributed at recess and they couldn't try them under any circumstances—these would be set ups, and we'd immediately recognize them as such. But it's completely unrealistic to tell kids that they must peacefully coexist at all times and never cross the line into persistent unfriendliness or name-calling or teasing or exclusion. There's no way 30 kids on a school bus are going to behave the way we want them to, day in and day out, without making some serious blunders. Children have to learn how to manage their aggressive impulses and get along, and they also have to learn to be resilient—these are *acquired* skills—and this is where the Zero Tolerance approach breaks down.

Social Emotional Learning and Zero Tolerance

Human beings have to learn almost everything in life. Anything that isn't instinctual is something we must master through learning. We have to learn to feed ourselves: how to use a spoon, then a fork, and then a knife. We have to learn how to use the toilet and tie our shoelaces. We have to learn how to tell time, ride a bike, and write a thank you note. We have to learn how to use good judgment when crossing the road, how to stand patiently in line, and how to share our toys. We have to learn to say *please* and *thank you* and *excuse me*, recognize letters of the alphabet, hold a pencil, and spell our names. None of these tasks comes naturally and *all* of them must be learned, and over time. And when it comes to aggression, everything we expect in terms of acceptable behavior must also be learned, and this includes skills such as impulse control, empathy, respect, good judgment, and resilience.

Indeed, the work of childhood is learning and mastering these skills (and many more), and we could reasonably argue that at the root of every incident we call bullying is a skill that hasn't yet been mastered. When considered in this way, the mistakes children make with one another are an important part of the learning curve—the social emotional learning curve.

Social Emotional Learning (SEL) is that part of the curriculum that governs the social and emotional aspects of childhood. According to SEL experts, social emotional skills include the following:

1. Recognizing emotions in self and others
2. Regulating and managing strong emotions (positive and negative)
3. Recognizing strengths and areas of need
4. Listening and communicating accurately and clearly
5. Taking others' perspectives and sensing their emotions
6. Respecting others and self and appreciating differences
7. Identifying problems correctly
8. Setting positive and realistic goals
9. Problem solving, decision making, and planning
10. Approaching others and building positive relationships
11. Resisting negative peer pressure
12. Cooperating, negotiating, and managing conflict nonviolently

13. Working effectively in groups

14. Help-seeking and help-giving

15. Showing ethical and social responsibility[7]

This is an incredible skill set, and it would be fair to characterize it as an anti-bullying skill set. You could also think of it as the skill set for the mastery of aggression.

Children (or adults) who possess and use these skills would be kind, patient, and compassionate independent thinkers. They could advocate for themselves, stick up for others, lend a helping hand, and be both great leaders and followers. With this skill set, children could do anything in life because they would have mastered the most important subject in their lives: themselves.

In truth, this skill set is as detailed and sophisticated as the skills required to do calculus or write an essay on the economic forces that con-tributed to the American Revolution, and like these other skills, the social emotional skills take a long time to master. This gets lost in our current discussions of childhood aggression: that it takes decades to master our-selves (and that maybe we never complete the process). Children must learn these skills in the same way they learn any other skill, and they must be taught as patiently and intentionally as any other subject. Children aren't going to behave in certain ways just because we want them to, in the same way they won't be able to play the piano well just because we want them to: they have to learn how to do it, and we have to teach them.

Let's consider for a moment how children learn, using mathematics as an example. To begin, children must be exposed to the subject early on, which means exposing them to numbers and prompting them to count. This is followed by the recognition and identification of written numbers, which kids generally grasp as a result of being read to. If they are consis-tently exposed to numbers, then by two or three children are able to hold up their fingers when asked their age. "Three!" they shout as they point their fingers in your face. "I'm three!" This is the beginning of learning math; the process doesn't start with the multiplication tables.

---

7. Kenneth W. Merrell, Ph.D., and Barbara A. Gueldner, Ph.D., "Social and emotional Learning in the Classroom: Promoting Mental Health and Academic Success" (*The Guilford Practical Intervention in School Series*, 2010).

Ideally children have acquired a lot of information about numbers and counting by the time they start school, but they need repeated and consistent exposure for this to occur. If the adults around them mentioned numbers just once a week, kids wouldn't learn much—you don't have to be an expert to recognize that such an approach wouldn't foster much development.

Once children start school, it's more of the same: consistent exposure. Go into any decent elementary classroom and *every day* there will be time dedicated to developing math skills. The same holds true for learning a foreign language—there's no way you can master it without practicing every day. If you want to develop true proficiency, you must speak, write, and read that language *all the time*. To master the skills of printing and cursive writing involves the same process—you must work on your skills almost every day. Repetition, repetition, repetition—one skill builds on another, and practice deepens understanding. In math, counting leads to addition and subtraction, then multiplication and division, then fractions, then algebra and geometry, which leads to calculus, and then to even higher levels of mathematics. There are no shortcuts to this process of learning, although children will acquire these skills at different rates depending on their level of interest.

In addition to exposure and repetition, educators and parents (parents being the primary educators of young children) understand that learning is a process that involves many mistakes. One of my favorite mistakes involving numbers occurred when my godson had just celebrated his third birthday. It was time for his annual physical check-up, and he was so excited about getting older, and so proud of being able to identify his age, that when the doctor asked him how old he was, he practically shouted, "I used to be three, but now I'm two!" He held up three fingers for the doctor as proof. Ah, yes, nobody's perfect. And this is the point. None of us starts out with all the answers. None of us acquires any skill without trying again and again and again, and none of us develops a sense of mastery without messing up mightily along the way.

Unfortunately, this is not the Zero Tolerance climate, and we can see evidence of this in various aspects of our approach to childhood aggression. The first is in the anti-bullying movement's attachment to Bully Language and labels, and with it an attention to what children should *not* be doing, rather than on what they should be doing. When a child is labeled as a bully, for example, this language doesn't point him to different behaviors or to the lessons he should learn. All it does is underscore his mistakes and convey the message that these mistakes define him. Imagine how my godson would have reacted if I had called him an idiot for getting his age wrong. Chances are he would have shut down and stopped trying, nipping in the bud his capacity for taking risks as a learner.

Those attached to Bully Language resist these kinds of comparisons on the grounds that in cases such as my godson's, the mistake didn't hurt anyone, so labeling him as an idiot isn't warranted. The reasoning then follows that a label such as bully *is* warranted because aggression can be intentional and hurtful. But this distinction doesn't matter when it comes to learning. Call a child an idiot and he's going to shut down. Call a child a bully and you'll get the same result. Neither labeled child will be motivated to figure out what they did wrong or to try to do better in the future.

The second way in which Zero Tolerance doesn't adhere to good learning practices is in the way it's delivered. The anti-bullying movement does not generally approach the topic of childhood aggression with the level of pedagogical sophistication and expertise that is necessary for real learning to occur. In fact, much of what is being done to combat childhood misbehavior doesn't come under the umbrella of teaching at all, and therefore it should come as no surprise that children don't seem to be learning the lessons we are trying to impart. An anti-bullying policy on a school website or a day-long seminar on anti-bullying strategies are not sufficient methods for shaping children's behavior. When we consider them to be sufficient we set children up to fail.

Finally, Zero Tolerance doesn't consider that children need to master different things at different stages of development, and each stage presents kids with new challenges. Let's keep these things in mind as we consider how most anti-bullying education works.

The following are some examples of the methods Zero Tolerance proponents suggest for dealing with bullying. We can think of these as the "lesson plans" we are delivering to our children.

1. *Include a prominent link to the school's bullying policy on your website.*

- *Review the highlights of the policy at back-to-school nights with families.*
- *Review the policy with students during the first week of school.*
- *Keep the conversation going about the zero tolerance for bullying policy that the school/district follows throughout the year.*
- *Consider having students, teachers, administrators, families. and vendors sign "contracts" or agreements that they've read the bullying policy and they pledge to adhere to this policy. Celebrate when students show acts of kindness, philanthropy or other social good. This isn't just about discipline and punishment, good anti-bullying practices include reward and recognition for doing the right thing![8]*

2. *Each school should establish a zero-tolerance policy toward bullying. Any student who feels he or she has been harassed verbally or physically, in person or via social media, should be able to file a complaint with the principal. The harassing student should be given a hearing before a committee of faculty members. If found guilty, the harassing student should be issued a notice of violation. Three notices of violation within a school year would result in the harassing student being expelled. The policy is clear. It is simple.[9]*

3. *Schools should have an entire day at the beginning of the school year dedicated to teaching what bullying is, what the consequences may be, teaching tolerance and compassion, ways to get help if bullied without repercussions. Simple, yet very powerful.[10]*

---

8. Creating a Zero Tolerance Environment, thebullyproject.com http://specialneeds.thebullyproject.com/zero_tolerance.

9.Chuck O'Neal, *Orlando Sentinel* online edition, October 11, 2011, http://articles.orlandosentinel.com/2011-10-11/news/os-ed-bullying-myword-101111-20111010_1_zero-tolerance-policy-student-social-media.

10. Caroline Cooper, TED Conversations, www.ted.com/conversations/1269/zero_tolerance_for_bullying_p.html.

Let's walk through these suggestions and see how they stack up from a learning perspective:

1. *Include a prominent link to the school's bullying policy on your website.*

    - *Review the highlights of the policy at back-to-school nights with families*
    - *Review the policy with students during the first week of school*

These initial suggestions are about disseminating some information; they're not about learning it. You can post information about the Pythagorean theorem on the website too, but this doesn't guarantee anyone will learn it. If we want to influence children's behavior, reviewing a policy with them during the first week of school is about as effective as giving them a lecture on multiplication and expecting them to walk away from it being able to multiply. Something on the website is fine, and reviewing won't hurt, but at best these are gestures that serve as reinforcement for what's being taught; they don't constitute teaching itself. One of the misconceptions underlying much of anti-bullying initiatives is that children should be able to understand really important information simply because we want them to understand it, and we confuse being emphatic with being effective.

Amidst this confusion, anti-bullying advocates conflate their desire for children to behave well with children's ability to do so. Because the subject of childhood aggression is so important, and because *we* understand it (or believe we do), many of us expect kids to appreciate its importance and to readily adopt our suggestions. But being emphatic is not enough.

2. *Keep the conversation going about the zero tolerance for bullying policy that the school/district follows throughout the year.*

A commitment to *keep the conversation going* is a step in the right direction, because it implies that more than just a one-shot approach is being used, but conversations in and of themselves aren't necessarily instructive. Kids wouldn't learn much about any other topic if they just had conversations about them. And, here, the suggestion is to have a *conversation* about a *policy.* Again, there isn't much real instruction happening here, so there won't be much learning as a result.

3. *Consider having students, teachers, administrators, families and vendors sign "contracts" or agreements that they've read the bullying policy and they pledge to adhere to this policy.*

A contract is a perfect Zero Tolerance tool. It is a legalistic approach to an issue that, in the case of childhood aggression, is essentially psychological and developmental in nature—an apples and oranges comparison if ever there was one. A contract makes sense in the case of bringing guns to school, for example, because the issue is already clear-cut; there is no middle ground, and there needn't ever be. Children don't have to learn how *not* to bring guns to school, so a contract makes perfect sense; it's not intended to be a learning tool, but this is what anti-bullying advocates want it to be.

By relying on a contract to shape children's behavior the assumption is that emphasizing a point constitutes sufficient education. If it were this simple when it comes to learning then kids would never make mistakes. They could sign contracts promising not to make any mistakes in all of their subjects. This argument seems specious if we assume that kids learn differently when it comes to aggression, but they don't. The process of learning is essentially the same no matter what the subject: exposure, repetition, practice, and making lots and lots of mistakes. In the end, for a contract to be meaningful and binding it must follow good educational practices. It can't be a substitute for them.

4. *Celebrate when students show acts of kindness, philanthropy, or other social good. This isn't just about discipline and punishment, good anti-bullying practices include reward and recognition for doing the right thing!*

These suggestions are definitely steps in the right direction because they point to the fact that children can't just be educated about what they shouldn't do, they must also be instructed about what they should do. My concern with anti-bullying education such as this is that it frames acceptable childhood behavior in light of bullying, which quickly brings us back to a fixed mindset.

5. *Each school should establish a zero-tolerance policy toward bullying. Any student who feels he or she has been harassed*

verbally or physically, in person or via social media, should be able to file a complaint with the principal. The harassing student should be given a hearing before a committee of faculty members. If found guilty, the harassing student should be issued a notice of violation. Three notices of violation within a school year would result in the harassing student being expelled. The policy is clear. It is simple.[11]

This is an example of what I call *education by fiat*. It is a declaration as much as anything. In order to make the point, the tone is unequivocal, and the policy leaves no margin for error or room for interpretation or context for those adhering to it. There will be a "hearing" and a "notice of violation," and there are only three strikes. But what if the first offense is egregious? Does this mean a student can remain in the community if he/she is a danger to others? What proponents of policies such as this seem to forget is that they cut both ways—if there's no room for maneuvering on one side (three strikes!), then there's no room for maneuvering on the other.

6. *Schools should have an entire day at the beginning of the school year dedicated to teaching what bullying is, what the consequences may be, teaching tolerance and compassion, ways to get help if bullied without repercussions. Simple, yet very powerful.*

This final suggestion clearly illustrates that many of our approaches to childhood aggression do not arise from an understanding of how children learn. *An entire day* of instruction in anything, no matter how important the subject, wouldn't make much of a dent, and we would be sorely disappointed if we expected kids to make lasting changes in their behavior based upon it. Whereas an entire day of instruction is too little, it is also, paradoxically, too much, educationally speaking. Children, especially young children, couldn't take in everything from an entire day of instruction in anything—it's way too much for them to absorb at once.

In addition, the above suggestion is about teaching many subtle and

---

11. Chuck O'Neal, *Orlando Sentinel* online edition, October 11, 2011, articles.orlandosentinel.com/2011-10-11/news/os-ed-bullying-myword-101111-20111010_1_zero-tolerance-policy-student-social-media.

profound things, such as tolerance and compassion. These are not things that can be learned in day, or in a workshop. Children learn to be compassionate when people show them compassion; they learn tolerance when others are tolerant of them. This knowledge seeps into them through experience, not as a result of a once-a-year, day-long lesson. And what about the kids who are absent from school that day?

The proponents of the Zero Tolerance approach get at least one thing right: it's simple. But it is patently ridiculous to think that such an approach could have a lasting impact on children and their behavior. This is just not how effective education works, largely because it doesn't target the underlying issues or present them in a way that is pedagogically sound. When children are instructed in a way that runs counter to how they learn and then are expected to have mastered what is being taught, they are being set up to fail.

This is Zero Tolerance at its worst: holding over children's heads the idea that they should behave in certain ways just because they've been told—not taught—to do so. According to the above suggestion, they are instructed once (however deliberately), in September, on the first day of school, when they are distracted and have ants in their pants and are reuniting with friends and getting back into the routine. As soon as they walk in the door they are subjected to a day-long seminar about all the things they can do wrong, all the ways they can get into trouble, all the ways they can feel hurt by other kids, and then they are expected to take this and run with it. *An entire day!* Would that adults could master all our challenges and solve all our problems so quickly and easily.

The above Zero Tolerance approaches not only disregard how children learn; they disregard principles of good teaching. I doubt there is a profession that is more misunderstood by outsiders than teaching. Many people have no idea what constitutes good teaching, and they assume that because teachers are woefully underpaid and underappreciated in our culture that it can't be *that* hard. Well, it is that hard, and instead of focusing their efforts on what children need to learn and how we can teach them, many anti-bullying advocates are instituting policies and laws in the hopes that they will do the work for them.

Anti-Bullying Policies and Legislation

Most schools and 49 states[12] have anti-bullying policies and legislation. School rules against harassment and violence aren't new, of course, but the specific rules against bullying are, as are the state anti-bullying laws. The first anti-bullying legislation was enacted in 1999 (in Georgia), with the majority of states passing legislation after 2005.[13] The fact that the oldest anti-bullying laws are barely a decade old underscores the point made in Chapter 1, which is that our attention to this issue, especially at the legislative level, is very new.

Many state laws simply require that school districts implement anti-bullying education programs and policies; these states leave it up to school districts to institute policies and procedures for dealing with bullying, including the punishment. Other states have taken a more proactive stance and have articulated specific consequences for bullying behavior. A few states have made bullying a misdemeanor, and legislators in at least one state (Rhode Island) want bullies to be dealt with as delinquents in family court. Hawaii has enacted very specific anti-bully legislation that states, "If any child of school age engages in bullying or cyberbullying, the child, and the father, mother, or legal guardian, shall be fined not more than $100 for each separate offense. Each day of violation shall constitute a separate offense."[14] And Massachusetts, in an effort to raise awareness about bullying, has declared that the fourth Wednesday in January is to be recognized as No Name Calling Day.

What is most extraordinary about all of this legislation is not any particular law but rather that, in the course of just a few years, and without data to support that there's been significant change in childhood behavior, our society has decided to deal with childhood aggression and misbehavior via the legal system. This is a radical departure from how childhood problems have been dealt with in the past. If nothing else, this wave of legislative activity should encourage us to take a very close look at how

---

12. With the exception of Montana, as of June, 2012.

13. Statistics from BullyPolice.org, www.bullypolice.org/.

14. www.capitol.hawaii.gov/session2010/bills/SB2094_.HTM.

our country's thinking about childhood is shifting and how this change of perspective is affecting how we respond to children.

When we rely on laws to regulate children's behavior, we are inclined to see those situations we wish to regulate, and children themselves, very differently than when we consider them from educational or developmental perspectives. By nature, laws are fairly clear cut and absolute—that's the purpose of a law—and this presumes that the problems the law is trying to address are also clear cut and absolute. In addition, the very existence of a law, like an observer in a scientific experiment, shapes what we see and how we understand the data before us. For example, anti-bullying laws are de facto declarations that *bully* is the appropriate label for a child who behaves in certain ways. With this presumption come other assumptions, such as that the dynamic between bully and victim is always a one-sided and one-dimensional interchange, and that the relationships are best regulated and mediated by law.

The existence of laws to regulate childhood behavior also means that misbehaving children are seen as lawbreakers, not merely as troublemakers, which no doubt affects our incentive to understand or have patience with those who need our guidance most. Note that Hawaii's law declares that any *school-aged* child can be found guilty of bullying, thus even very young misbehaving children are capable of being outlaws.

In addition, once laws have been instituted, there is much less room for error on the part of the child. In Hawaii, for example, the legislation presumes that children should be able to learn their lesson in a day, as each subsequent day of misbehavior under the law constitutes an additional violation. By this way of thinking—which completely defies all reasoning when it comes to learning and development—kids should be able to change overnight and, really, that only a state of perfection is acceptable. In addition, this thinking presumes that a punishment, one that is completely divorced from the infraction—such as a fine—will have a positive and lasting effect on a young child. *In a day.*

So, make no mistake, children are now being held accountable for their mistakes not just by rules and developmentally appropriate discipline, which is how the rest of us were raised, but by the rule of law.

The Value of Mistakes

This is proof that the Zero Tolerance position doesn't appreciate the value of mistakes, or the role mistakes play in effective education. One of the realities of learning—and this includes social emotional learning, of course—is that mistakes are inevitable. Contrary to what the enactment of all these laws would suggest, mistakes don't indicate that children haven't worked hard enough, or don't want to be good, or aren't headed in the right direction, but this is what Zero Tolerance legislation would have us believe. Mistakes are critical to learning, and if children are given the idea that they should never make mistakes, then any educational initiative will fail, plain and simple. This doesn't mean children should not be held accountable for their behavior or be guided by rules and consequences and punishments, but it does mean mistakes are an inevitable and essential part of learning, and expectations about outcomes should be aligned accordingly.

I once worked with a group of 7th grade girls that had been instructed to write letters of apology to someone whom they thought they had mistreated. The lesson was about decision-making and regret, and the point of the exercise was not to actually send the letters (although the kids were free to do so) but rather for the students to reflect upon their actions and consider how their behavior affected others. In reading over the letters, I came across one from a girl named Tanya, who addressed her letter to a former classmate, a girl she had gone to school with in 5th grade. Tanya told the girl she was sorry for all the nasty e-mails she had sent and the mean things she had said to her. She apologized for excluding the girl from her social group. Tanya explained that, at the time, she didn't realize how unkind her comments and actions were but now, with some perspective, she could see how hurtful her behavior must have been.

Tanya demonstrated with her letter that she had learned an incredible lesson. She was able to understand, via a process of guided reflection, that there were times when she behaved in ways that were unacceptable. With the benefit of hindsight, and by putting herself in her classmate's shoes, she was able to understand how powerful her words and actions were and that she could affect other people deeply.

Mark Twain's quote, *Good judgment comes from experience, and experience comes from bad judgment* proved true in Tanya's case. Her bad judgment with her friend became an experience that, once she had the chance to reflect upon it, guided her to better judgment. By the time I knew her, Tanya was one of the kindest, most compassionate kids in her class. She set the tone for decency and good judgment (at a 7th grade level) among her group of friends. She was keenly aware of the feelings of others and often based her decisions on how they would affect the group as a whole.

Tanya was a joy to work with but, by her own account, she hadn't been so good just a few years earlier (at least not to one girl in particular). What made her a different kid in the 7th grade than she had been in 5th grade was her experience, which had informed her ideas about herself and others. Tanya still had many lessons to learn but she was on the right path, and she had her experience to thank for it.

Adults naturally want to help children avoid making mistakes, especially the ones that might hurt the feelings of another child. But many anti-bullying advocates now expect kids to be perfect in this regard—to never make social emotional mistakes—and, more to the point, to never feel pain, which is fueling our obsession with bullying. They want the Tanyas of the world (who are every kid) to learn their lesson the easy way, and they are convinced that they can make this happen by sending the Zero Tolerance message about mistakes.

Research shows that kids who fear making mistakes become risk averse, and this is problematic because risk-taking goes hand in hand with learning. The brain develops by taking risks, by doing new things, by stretching itself, and it can only do these things successfully if it is relieved of the burden of messing up. If mistakes are presented to children as being bad, wrong, always preventable, and as a reflection of their character, then kids will shut down and stop trying. If mistakes are presented as being part of the process, something to learn from, and not a reflection of character, then kids embrace learning. Luckily for her, Tanya understood mistakes in this latter way, which is what allowed her to go back and reflect upon her mistakes so successfully. Had she been taught that mistakes were always preventable and thus a negative and permanent reflection on her, she would have felt too much shame to actually learn something from her experience.

When I explain this to parents, they sometimes make the distinction between what they see as positive risk-taking, such as kids stretching themselves academically, and negative risk-taking, such as kids testing out behaviors and boundaries with friends. They want kids to take risks in one area and not in the other and still learn the appropriate lessons. I understand this, but it doesn't hold up with how children learn, and this is the thrust behind Zero Tolerance, the idea that kids should be able to learn certain lessons without making mistakes.

Zero Tolerance and Resilience

When we see the world through the Zero Tolerance lens, in addition to downplaying the value of mistakes, we completely discount the importance of resilience. Focusing on resilience isn't necessary when there is such a divide between right and wrong, innocence and guilt. A victim has no need to think about building resilience when the responsibility for his/her pain rests solely in the hands of the bully. Because the Zero Tolerance philosophy considers childhood aggression such a one-sided affair, only the bully needs our attention in terms of growth, and only the bully must learn something from his/her actions.

Broaching the topic of resilience with Zero Tolerance advocates is akin to blaming the victim, and it is, as long as we use the label of victim and accept childhood aggression as a categorically one-sided proposition. From this perspective, speaking of resilience is insulting to victims, and any resilience that results for the victim isn't seen as a positive outcome but rather as something that should have been avoided in the first place, regardless of any benefit. In this way, Zero Tolerance does not value resilience; it values victimhood, however inadvertently. In the denial of the importance of resilience, Zero Tolerance leads children to identify with being victims, and they learn that their power lies in embracing their pain, not in moving through challenges.

Resilience is about moving through and moving on—it's about growth and development. Zero Tolerance, as much as it aims to solve problems, has little tolerance for how problems are effectively solved, and how much we must consider development when we deal with the problem of childhood aggression.

Childhood Development

Zero Tolerance is essentially a one-size-fits-all approach to dealing with childhood aggression, and what's most troubling is that it doesn't sufficiently acknowledge childhood development in its policies and responses to problems between children.

Let's return to the suggestion of a daylong anti-bullying workshop and see what this means. It sounds like the idea is for all students to attend the seminar, which on one level makes sense, if you want everyone to get the same message, but let's assume that we're talking about a K-8 school, or even just an elementary school (grades K-5). This is a huge range of kids, spanning in age from five to 11 years old. Having the goal of delivering the same message at the same time, and in the same manner, to all of the kids is totally unrealistic.

A child's capacity to hear the message—any message—and to learn something from it varies depending on his/her age and stage of development. Delivering the same message to all middle-school students (grades 6-8) is a stretch because so much happens developmentally between these years. How a 6th grader and an 8th grader comprehend the same lesson will differ enormously, which means that, in order to be relevant, the lesson itself must differ for each separate cohort. The fact that we want the outcome to be the same with all kids (*no bullying!*) doesn't mean the lesson can be the same, not if we want it to be effective.

It is around the issue of development that the supposed simplicity and clarity of the Zero Tolerance approach breaks down. As the above Zero Tolerance suggestions demonstrate, these approaches are generally, and perhaps unknowingly, targeted at a certain developmental range of child. For example, the suggestion of having everyone read through an anti-bullying policy and sign a contract makes absolutely no sense—and would be completely ineffective—for young children. The average first grader, for example, does not have the ability to comprehend the language or intent of a policy, therefore having her sign a contract is meaningless. Even the concept of a contract is sophisticated and well beyond the capacity of kids this age to understand. Having an older teenager sign a contract, on the other hand, is an entirely different matter, and it could be a meaningful gesture if presented in the right way.[15]

Here's another way to think about contracts: if a 7-year-old were to sign a contract of any other kind, and then violate it, the contract wouldn't hold up in an actual court. Why? Because the kid is only seven! This analogy may seem far-fetched but if the Zero Tolerance movement is going to co-opt concepts such as contracts from the legal profession— and go so far as to institute laws—then it should follow its own logic through to its natural conclusion. Children don't fully grasp the purpose or ramifications of contracts when it comes to other areas of life, but this fact seems to be overlooked by the Zero Tolerance boosters when it comes to childhood aggression. This is a grave mistake, and it indicates that they don't appreciate the role development plays when it comes to kids, their behavior, and accountability. Indeed, the issue of development is key to understanding and dealing with childhood aggression and there doesn't seem to be much consideration of it when it comes to Zero Tolerance.

In the following pages I will examine essential aspects of two stages of school-aged development: elementary school (ages 5-10) and middle school (ages 11-14). This is not intended to be a comprehensive guide to childhood development but rather an overview of the aspects of development that are most relevant to our consideration of childhood aggression and our methods of dealing with it. When we adopt Zero Tolerance toward childhood aggression, we are actually demonstrating little tolerance for the legitimate and normal phases of childhood.

Development and The Elementary School Child

Schooling begins for most children at about age 5, with kindergarten. For some children, this is the first time they have been away from home and in large groups with other kids, and for others it's the first time they've had to follow a program that goes beyond simple play. It is an exciting time for both children and their parents, but it can also be fraught with anxiety as children face the first major requirements of formal education:

---

15. In fact, most teenagers do sign contracts. Obtaining a driver's license is a contract of sorts, in that the 16-year-old who receives one agrees to abide by the rules of the road and accept the consequences for not doing so.

paying attention, following directions, behaving consistently, and getting along with a large number of other children.

This last item is particularly relevant to aggression because school is mandatory, and children have no choice about their classmates: they must deal with one another whether they like it not. This means there is ample opportunity for disagreement and conflict. In addition, by the time children enter kindergarten, they are capable of playing *with* each other, not just alongside each other (when they're young, kids engage in something called parallel play), and this means there are even more opportunities for conflict.

So this is where it begins.

I recently spoke with a mother who reported that a classmate bullied her daughter when she was younger. She didn't get into the specifics; she said only that the girl who bullied her daughter was "toxic" and a "ring leader." She spoke of the girl's unremitting meanness and how much she terrorized her daughter. According to this mother, this girl had no redeeming qualities, and her behavior in particular was willful and damaging. When I asked how old her daughter was when this dynamic occurred, the mother replied, "Six years old—they were in first grade."

People routinely tell me stories like this, and I could swear that the children who are identified as bullies are getting younger and younger every year (the youngest bully I've heard about was three years old). This, of course, reinforces our belief that we've got an epidemic on our hands. If we honestly believe these very young children are capable of committing such horrible acts, then of course we assume our country is going to hell in a handbasket. But before we go that route, and accept the characterizations of these children as accurate (let alone label them as bullies), we need to consider what their brains and minds are capable of at these young ages and factor their development into our understanding of them.

Intent

Perhaps the most important thing we must consider is the issue of intent. By intent I mean the degree to which young children possess the capacity for things such as forethought, anticipation, planning, willfulness, and empathy when it comes to hurting one another. Intent is an ingredient that completely alters the flavor of an interaction between children and transforms a mild interaction into something that's too hot to handle. When kids misbehave but don't possess intent to do harm, we tend to think of them as misbehaving children. When kids misbehave with intent, we are much more inclined to consider them bullies. Intent, therefore, is central to our understanding of what we term bullying.

A child's capacity for intent is very different than an adult's. One of the reasons many adults are so alarmed about childhood aggression is because they project onto children a level of intent that children simply don't possess, and adults do this because they don't understand development. A classic adult mistake is to believe that kids think like we do and that their capacity for intent is the same as ours. We see evidence of this lack of understanding in how Zero Tolerance advocates propose to educate kids about aggression (see above), so it stands to reason that this lack of understanding extends to issues such as intent as well.

The mother who thought her daughter had been bullied ascribed terrible motives (i.e. intent) to the child who supposedly hurt her daughter, and this determined how she dealt with the situation. She was convinced that the girl had it out for her daughter, that she willingly and repeatedly targeted her daughter, and that it was her goal to make her daughter feel bad. She assumed all of the girl's behavior was calculated and she repeatedly spoke with her daughter about the girl's maliciousness. Understandably, the daughter came to understand the situation in the same way as her mother, and so, after a while, all of the girl's behavior was cloaked in malicious intent for both mother and daughter.

Now, I have no doubt that this young girl felt bad at times during her relationship with this classmate. But I have many doubts about the motivation of the offending child. Kids can be really mean to each other—even really little kids can be really mean—but we must understand that meanness in a six-year-old is vastly different than meanness in an adult, and yet this mother couldn't see the difference. Because her daughter felt pain, the mother assumed the cause must be something that was premeditated, targeted, and intentional.

If we pause for a moment to consider children's capacity for premeditation, targeting, and intention in other areas of their lives a clearer picture emerges. Six-year-olds can't anticipate much, nor can they plan very well, so to assume that a six-year-old can plan and execute a campaign of targeted meanness against another child is a big leap. Kids this age live in the moment, and their glimpses of the future certainly don't involve planning much for it. This means we shouldn't confuse a child's anticipation for an upcoming event (*It's my birthday next week! I want ice cream for dessert!*) with the ability to plan every detail of a birthday party or purchase an ice cream cone on their own.

Speaking of birthday parties, I know many people who think that not inviting a child to a birthday party is the sort of mean-spirited behavior that constitutes bullying (because it's social exclusion). In reality, though, a young child who doesn't want another child at a birthday party is really just expressing an opinion, not deliberately calculating ways to hurt the feelings of the uninvited child. This seems lost on many adults because *we* know what it means to leave someone off the guest list. If we did such a thing, it might be an indication of our intention to hurt someone's feelings, and we project onto children this degree of intention and social sophistication.

When a child expresses that she doesn't want to invite a certain child to her party, this is a great opportunity for adults to explain how this might make the other child feel. Such an explanation may not make a difference to the birthday girl, but it's a start. It's not the time, however, to see the birthday girl as malicious or determined to beat down the spirits of the other child, even if she sticks to her guns and reiterates her desire for her peer to be left off the invite list and even if she agrees that such behavior on her part might be mean. Such an acknowledgement on the part of the birthday girl still doesn't constitute the degree of calculation many adults believe it to be—the birthday girl is allowed to not want a peer at her party without this being a sign that she's plotting for the peer's downfall.

Once again, I'm not saying young kids can't be mean; they can be. What they can't do is think ahead about most things, such as consistently anticipate how another child might feel. To presume that they can is unrealistic. The way some parents talk about young "bullies," such as the mother above, you'd think kids were plotting and scheming against their victims all day long. Well, they're not, because they can't; their limited attention span guarantees it.

To repeat: young kids can't plot or scheme about much in advance, so their bad behavior, when it is directed towards peers, is generally situational rather than premeditated, meaning it arises in response to a given situation. And even if the same situation presents itself repeatedly, it doesn't mean young children can calculate to the degree adults presume they can. This is a very hard point to convince some parents of, especially if they believe their child is suffering at the hands of a peer. It's also a point lost on many legislators and policymakers. When a school-aged child can be found guilty of a misdemeanor, then it is clear we are attributing to children a level of cognitive functioning that they do not possess.

With these projections now come adult-like consequences, such as levying fines. But to what end? Not only do six-year-olds not earn money, they don't really understand the value of money, so this provision of the law (at least in Hawaii) is utterly meaningless, both as a tool of punishment and as one of education. A much more appropriate consequence would be taking away a child's favorite toy for a while, but we have lost sight of this. Besides, the courts can't regulate this kind of punishment. Now that many adults believe children's capacity for intent matches their own, children have to be dealt with in the same way—by law. However, it is both foolish and unproductive to create adult consequences for childhood misbehavior. When we do so we do nothing more than trumpet our own ignorance.

Development and The Middle-school child

Middle school is not an easy time.[16] There's probably not a person on the planet that would willingly go back to middle school, let alone look back on middle school as the high point of their childhood. It's no wonder that bullying, as we currently define it, runs rampant during this time. There are very good reasons for this. One of them is the amount of change that occurs in all aspects of a child's life during this time, and how much kids must learn and adapt to these changes throughout this period of their lives.

---

16. For the purposes of this discussion, I define middle school as grades 6-8, which translates into ages 11-14 (but can dip as low as age 10 and as high as age 15).

To give you a sense of how much transformation takes place during middle school, imagine a longitudinal lineup of all middle school students, ranging on the one end from 6th graders at the beginning of September to 8th graders at the end of June on the other, and you would see an evolution on the physical, emotional, and cognitive scales no less dramatic than the transition from the Neanderthal to *homo sapiens*. And this transformation gets packed into less than three years—no wonder it isn't pretty.

Given this amount of change, it isn't surprising that studies suggest bullying is most prevalent during the middle school years. This also makes sense given our expanded definition of it, which includes behaviors such as name-calling, teasing, and social exclusion, which are behaviors that flourish in middle school.[17] The prevalence of so-called bullying makes sense given what we know about development. Middle school is a time of extraordinary upheaval for kids. When parents complain to me about the behavior of their middle-school children (and they routinely do), I remind them that their kids go through more change in a day than adults do in a month, and that if parents had to do what middle-schoolers do all day long, then they'd be moody, unpredictable, uncooperative, nasty, snarky, and mean too.

Here's a quick reminder about what middle school is like for those of you who have forgotten your own experience.

School Changes

Middle school has a very different curriculum and flow than elementary school, and students have to adjust to more teachers, more movement throughout the day (for example, switching classes rather than having just one teacher), and often bigger class sizes. Many school districts have distinct middle schools where children must start at an entirely new school once they complete elementary school. This means new routines, new rhythms, new faces (often several elementary schools funnel into one middle school), and learning a new school culture.

Children are expected to have mastered reading, writing, and basic math skills during elementary school so that by the time they reach middle

---

17. antibullyingprograms.org/Statistics.html.

school they can begin the process of learning how to think analytically and abstractly. This is a huge challenge and it takes years to complete, but kids must keep pace. When they have problems, they fall behind quicker in middle school than they did in elementary school because there's more on their plate. Homework loads increase significantly and kids (at least the ones who do their work) start to feel the pressure.

I once worked with a 6th grade girl whose teacher was concerned that she was really hard on herself and stressed-out about her work. The girl was vigilant about her studies and never felt good enough. When I asked her about this, she replied, "I have to work hard so I can get into a good college, and then I need to get into a good medical school so I can become a surgeon and make a lot of money and take care of my parents." Some parents hear this and think, *why can't my kid be like that,* but this girl's attitude reflected a level of concern and stress about the future that younger kids simply don't possess. On the other end of the spectrum is the student who reaches middle school and feels daunted by the increased expectations and gives up; it's the flip side of the same coin.

By middle school, students have the cognitive capacity to understand the future in a new way. They live less in the moment than younger kids do, which may be one of the most significant differences. Younger kids, for the most part, are creatures of the moment; their worlds are mostly about the present. For middle schoolers, things start to shift and they can consider the past and look toward the future in new ways. This adds a new dimension to their experience, and brings with it the potential for the kind of introspection and angst that is typical of the teenage years. Thinking about the past and the future sets the stage for existential thoughts in adolescence, which can cause middle school kids to feel moody and uncertain.

Emotional Changes

Emotions run high during this time in a child's life. They are like cloud bursts: sudden, dramatic, and often accompanied by lots of precipitation. The child who was an even-keeled youngster can become a moody, petulant child in middle school through no fault of his own.

I frequently explain to parents that one of the biggest tasks for middle school kids is to keep it together during the school day so as to maintain a good appearance for their peers. Kids will do almost anything to avoid embarrassing themselves in front of their friends—and even more so their enemies—and this includes putting a clamp on their emotions. This is hard to do, especially when their emotions run all over the place. In fact, keeping emotions under control takes a massive amount of psychological energy and effort.

This explains, in part, why kids can be so nasty to their parents when they see them at the end of the school day. A parent's innocent inquiry, such as *How was school today, Honey?* can set off a cascade of negative emotions in the child, and the resulting purge can leave parents feeling shocked, bruised and battered. A typical parent refrain is *I hope you don't talk to your teachers like that* and, for the most part, the answer is no, they don't, and this is the salient point. Adolescents save their worst selves for the people who love them, who won't judge them like their peers do, and who don't care if they look/sound/act cool. The rest of the time, they expend enormous amounts of their psychic energy on trying to fit in and not drawing negative attention to themselves.

But their inner worlds remain volcanic, and they can blow at any moment. This means that adolescents routinely overreact to things, and I can't emphasize this point enough. I joke with parents that middle school is all about *drama and trauma* because this is what the red-hot emotions make kids feel—every issue and problem and interchange is larger-than-life to them, and when it's negative it's really, really bad.

I once spent an hour talking to a heartbroken boy who was lamenting the loss of his first girlfriend. He went on and on (and on) about his upset, and described his feelings of abandonment and pain in exquisite detail. He read me the letters he had written to her and never sent, and the letters she had written to him. He told me that the relationship was the most wrenching of his life. He painted a picture of true love cut short, a tragedy of Shakespearean proportion, and I'll admit it—I got caught up in the whole thing (especially because boys don't usually expound on this sort of stuff). It all sounded so painful and poignant, so raw and yet so beautiful at the same time. Ah yes, I thought, this is what love is all about. But when the boy began to repeat himself, I asked him how long the relationship had lasted. "A week," he replied.

There you have it. That's the emotional world of the average middle schooler.

Zara's experience provides another example of the emotions of early adolescence. During a long weekend, Zara, an 8th grader, spent two nights sleeping over at a friend's house with a large group of other girls. When her mother told her she couldn't sleep over for a third night, Zara became hysterical. She cried continuously for two hours—sobbing, heaving, and moaning non-stop. At one point, her mother thought her daughter was going to hyperventilate. Her mother had never seen Zara so out of control, and nothing she did seemed to help. She was simply inconsolable, and eventually Zara cried herself to sleep.

Zara's mother assumed her daughter was upset because she didn't get what she wanted, but the next morning, once Zara had regained her composure, she explained to her mom that in fact she was upset by the thought of being excluded from her group of friends. To her this meant being out of the loop, missing out on gossip, or maybe even being the subject of gossip because of her absence. By missing just one night with her friends, Zara feared she would be absent from Facebook photos and private jokes, and the prospect of this exclusion made her feel distraught.

So whether it's a broken heart or not being able to attend a sleepover, young adolescents feel the pain acutely, and this pain looks like overreaction to those of us not caught up in the same emotional maelstrom. Of course, young adolescents like Zara don't think they're overreacting; their pain and perspectives are very real to them. They aren't faking it; nevertheless *we* know that being absent from a sleepover is not the end of the world. I wouldn't put it this way to a middle schooler who was in pain because at best it wouldn't help and, at worst, it would be uncaring and unkind. But I also wouldn't respond to them in a way that would validate that missing a sleepover *did* mark the end of the world.

Another side effect of strong emotions in young adolescents is a feeling of victimization. When her mother prevented her from attending the sleepover, Zara was convinced no one could possibly understand her pain; no one else had ever had to deal with such a terrible situation. Her suffering felt unique and unparalleled. This was also the case of the heartbroken boy. It didn't help him to know that most people go through the same thing. To him, his suffering was singular and epic. No one had suffered as he suffered and, therefore, no one understood. Both kids were unable to see beyond their own experiences, so their pain took on a larger-than-life quality to them.

This feeling of uniqueness among kids this age contributes to the perception that they are being targeted when they feel great pain. When they are in the midst of their emotional trials, young adolescents can't see beyond their own suffering, and this self-absorption leads them to believe that the world is conspiring against them.

Physical Changes

Not only do young adolescents feel as though the world is conspiring against them, they sometimes feel their bodies are conspiring against them, too, and for good reason. Those of us who work in schools are reminded each September of how much change takes place during this time when returning students appear to have morphed into new beings in just a few short months. The physical transformation is indeed remarkable. From new body hair to menstruation to acne to weight gain to growth spurts to body odor to breaking voices to spontaneous erections—the list of changes seems endless, and they take time getting used to.

Beyond catapulting young adolescents out of childhood, this process also ensures that kids remain singularly focused on themselves. There is so much happening, and so many things to adapt to, that it would be impossible for kids *not* to be self-absorbed during this time.

Self-Consciousness

This self-absorption also means that middle-school kids are intensely self-conscious, and this makes sense given what's going on in their bodies. How would you feel if you didn't know what you were going to see in the mirror from one day to the next? As adults, we rely on a degree of predictability in our lives; young adolescents don't have this luxury, and the enormous and rapid changes they are going through cause them to be intensely self-involved and self-absorbed.

Ben's situation drives home this point. Ben had just started 6th grade at a new school. Many of his classmates already knew each other but Ben didn't know a soul, which made him feel even more self-conscious than usual. One day at lunch, Ben violated one of the rules of conduct in the cafeteria without knowing it (he took food outside of the designated eating area). In an effort to send a message to all students, the teacher in charge decided to make an example of Ben's transgression by giving a consequence to *all* the students. The students were denied a small privilege for a week and Ben was mortified, even though most of his classmates didn't know he was the one who broke the rule in the first place.

I got a call from Ben's mother a few days later. She reported that Ben had refused to go to school the day after the incident and that each morning since he had complained of a stomachache and asked to stay home. She said Ben told her he wanted to transfer to another school and that he feared he would be targeted for his mistake and ostracized for the rest of middle school. His assessment was that he wouldn't be able to recover from this incident and that he should just admit defeat now.

I explained to Ben's mother that his reaction was predictable given his age, and the good news was that *everybody* felt as self-conscious as Ben did. This meant that nobody would remember the event in a few days. Despite the fact that adolescents feel as though they are the center of the universe, they're not—they're only the center of their own universe—and this serves them well in situations like Ben's. By the following week, no one seemed to recall what had happened. There were new dramas to pay attention to and Ben's mistake was old news.

Consider how this level of self-consciousness plays out in other areas of life for young adolescents. When they feel self-conscious about their bodies, for instance, they believe everyone else will notice their perceived imperfections. I once dealt with a 7th grade girl who didn't want to go to school because she had a huge pimple on her nose—she was convinced her zit would be the topic of everyone's conversation. She failed to appreciate that almost all of her classmates had big pimples on their faces too, and that they were as consumed by their own feelings of self-consciousness as she was. Sadly, the young adolescent brain doesn't usually feel reassured by knowing that painful experiences are common to others. Instead, they feel burdened and isolated by their perceived differences. The worst thing that can happen to them is to stand out in a negative way.

It's the same thing when they feel too stupid or too smart—they don't want to stand out in a way that draws any unwanted attention. This explains, in part, why they can be inconsolable, because rational arguments against their emotional state make no sense to them.

The following is an example of adolescent self-consciousness that's hard for even the most compassionate adults to appreciate, despite the fact that it almost paralyzed the girl experiencing it. Carrie and Gail, both 12, planned to take the bus to the mall to hang out with other friends. As they were standing at the bus top, Carrie noticed that Gail was wearing a new pair of shoes, a style that Carrie had never seen before and judged to be incredibly ugly. "What are *those*?" Carrie demanded. Gail explained these were a style of shoe that everyone in another country was wearing, a place she had recently visited. "Aren't they great?" Gail boasted. Carrie was unconvinced. She couldn't believe Gail would willingly leave the house wearing something so unacceptable, and she feared other people would judge her harshly based on Gail's shoes. As they rode the bus in silence, Carrie wondered if she could beg off the trip to the mall by pretending she didn't feel well. She was so consumed with self-consciousness that she was sure other people on the bus were staring at Gail's shoes and, in turn, judging her by association.

Adults often dismiss these kinds of adolescent concerns out of hand because *they* no longer feel this way (thank goodness!) and therefore it's hard for them to put themselves back into this mindset. They don't think their friends' shoes reflect upon them, and they can snap out of it if they are concerned about a blemish on their faces. Adolescents can't do this yet. To them, a huge zit is an all-consuming affair, at least until the next all-consuming affair comes along—such as a friend's pair of shoes. It's easy for adults to mistake these obsessions as an indication of shallowness or vanity on the adolescent's part, but they're not. They are, in fact, the struggles of the nascent self, trying to figure out who it is; they are the undulations of the psychological chrysalis as it prepares to emerge in different form.

Self-consciousness not only leaves kids feeling vulnerable, it also primes them to be on the attack. Chances are good that the girl with the pimple would have been the first to notice someone else's pimple. And rather than feeling comforted by knowing someone else was going through what she was, she might have pointed out the other person's pimple as a way to deflect attention from her own situation. This, in turn, would have made her feel even worse about herself. Being critical of others can initially make kids feel better about themselves but this relief is short lived and it only serves to compound their negative feelings. In this way, adolescent self-consciousness not only belies insecurity, it breeds it. It's like a negative feedback loop that churns away in the psyche of those poor souls trapped between childhood and adulthood.

Finally, self-consciousness makes adolescents take things personally. For example, Elena, a 7th grader, was convinced that her homeroom teacher hated her. The teacher had never said anything specific to Elena about her behavior—and she had never spoken with her parents—nevertheless, Elena was certain that when the teacher made comments to the class about its behavior she was the intended target. When the teacher got exasperated with her students (something that happens to even the best teachers), Elena believed the teacher was really exasperated only with her. "She hates me," Elena complained to me, "I just know it."

"How do you know it?" I asked. "I just do," Elena replied. "She always singles me out and tells everyone what I'm doing wrong. She doesn't do this to anyone else—just to me. She totally hates me."

I happened to know Elena's teacher well. I had observed her class many times and watched her trying to herd the 7th grade cats. I also knew her style of dealing with problems. She spoke with the student directly and then contacted the school administration and the student's parents, if necessary. When Elena reported that none of these things had occurred, I was pretty sure she had misread the situation. I even went so far as to speak with Elena's teacher and asked her if she had any concerns about Elena. "Are you kidding me?" she asked. "Elena's great. I wish I had more students like her."

Which brings us to what's happening in the early adolescent brain.

Cognitive Changes

The brain of the young adolescent child is undergoing major changes. What is most important to understand, as we consider adolescent behavior, is what's happening in two separate parts of the brain: the frontal lobes and the amygdala.

The Frontal Lobes

The frontal lobes are the parts of the brain that house the executive functions. The executive functions include: reasoning, problem solving, the capacity for anticipation and judgment, planning, impulse control, inhibition, and attention. All of these functions are still very much under construction in the adolescent brain, and sometimes they work better than at other times. Even when one function performs reasonably well, all functions commonly don't operate in sync all the time, leaving the adolescent prone to making all kinds of missteps.

Throughout adolescence the developing brain learns how to recruit all of the executive functions when needed; it coordinates them into a coherent system that eventually allows adolescents to be independent and successful once they arrive at adulthood. But this takes many years to accomplish and many hurdles accompany every gain.[18] Regardless of how well intentioned or intelligent a child is, there is no rushing this process of transformation. Even the brightest, most well-behaved kids must develop their executive functions through trial and error. Imagine a football team trying to coordinate a play without a quarterback and you'll get the picture of how the executive functions work in the adolescent brain. It can be mayhem.

Consider impulse control and judgment. An obvious example of lack of impulse control is when children can't sit still—when they fidget and poke each other, things of this nature. But a less obvious example can be found in how kids communicate. Middle-school kids are not known for their discretion, and a lot of this has to do with impulse control, not just with their desire for gossip. They blurt out whatever is on their minds, regardless of how negative or mean it might be. Couple this with poor judgment, and you have the child who goes onto Facebook and says nasty things about another child.

A Florida mother didn't take this into consideration when she choked a 14-year-old boy whom she believed had bullied her daughter on Facebook.[19] Apparently the boy had made some mean comments in

---

18. According to neurologists, the brain doesn't reach developmental maturity until age 25.

19. *Yahoo News,* June 4, 2012, www.news.yahoo.com/blogs/abc-blogs/florida-mom-arrested-choking-14-old-bully-offers-135330347—abc-news-topstories.html.

response to a picture her daughter had posted. The woman, 46, seeing the boy in the local mall, approached him and, "I lost my temper," she said, by way of explaining why she wrapped her hands around the boy's throat and screamed expletives at him. "I wish it would have been another route I had taken. I don't go around doing that to children. I don't want to sound like I'm a huge monster."

The headline of the story read: Mom Regrets Choking Facebook Bully.

I don't go around doing that to children, and yet this is precisely what she did, and then she went onto national television to talk about it. Not surprisingly, she didn't want anyone to think she was a monster; she wanted everyone to think a 14-year-old boy was a monster. She justified her behavior by explaining how the boy was so thoughtless and mean, and then she turned around and behaved in the same manner, except she added physical force to her mistakes.

Once you understand development, you can't fairly compare the actions of a 14-year-old boy and those of a 46-year-old woman. They are categorically different because the 14-year-old's brain is not yet fully developed and therefore it is prone to making mistakes, like saying inappropriate things on Facebook. The 46-year-old's brain, on the other hand, *should* be developed enough to find better ways to deal with its aggression than to impulsively choke a child. It's not enough for us to follow these sorts of actions with statements such as, "I want people to, obviously, try to go through the proper channels," as the woman did.

This kind of self-serving sentiment underscores the hypocrisy that is being promulgated by our culture's bullying mania, and it illustrates how little issues of development are being taken into consideration. Had this woman afforded the boy in question one tenth of the amount of leeway she gave herself, she would have forgiven him and invested her energy into helping her daughter deal with her feelings.

Facial Expressions

Another area in which the adolescent brain is still developing is in its ability to read facial expressions. Kids at this age do not have an adult capacity for detecting subtleties in facial expressions, and if we return to Elena's case from above we can see what this looks like.

Elena, as you will recall, was convinced that her teacher hated her, and she based this conviction on her teacher's supposed behavior. What Elena was actually responding to, however, was not her teacher's behavior but her facial expressions—remember, the teacher never actually said or did anything to indicate that she was upset with Elena. Elena was reacting to her teacher's face and she was responding to her own misreading of her teacher's expressions. If the teacher frowned, then Elena believed she was angry—and angry with Elena, in particular. If the teacher expressed exasperation, then Elena assumed the teacher hated her. Not only did Elena take all of the teacher's facial cues personally, she got them wrong. Of course, Elena's interpretations weren't entirely out of the ballpark but they were considerably exaggerated, which lead her to make false assumptions about her teacher's intentions.

The Amygdala

Another part of the brain we must attend to when understanding the behavior of young adolescents is the amygdala, that area of the brain that regulates the fight-or-flight response. The fight-or-flight system is what alerts us to danger, both real and imagined. When we feel threatened in any way, this part of our brain kicks in and our heart rate and blood pressure increases; we become more vigilant and our bodies prepare for action. The fight-or-flight response keep us safe because it makes sure we take action before danger strikes, but it can work against us when we see danger in all kinds of places.

In this way, the amygdala plays a critical role in the social life of the young adolescent. For instance, researchers have demonstrated that young adolescent girls in particular fear social exclusion more than almost anything else.[20] Not being invited to a party, feeling shunned by peers, or even feeling left out of some gossip can create in them the perception of danger and the activation of a fight-or-fight response ensues. Given this neurological and physiological reality, Zara's above-mentioned response to not being allowed to attend a sleepover with her friends is understandable. She really felt like she was in danger when her mother

---

20. Data presented by Abigail Baird, Ph.D., Associate Professor of Psychology, Vassar College, Learning and the Brain Conference, Cambridge, MA, 2005.

foiled her plans, and her nervous system went into overdrive. She wasn't being an ungrateful brat; she was panicked because she felt like her social world was collapsing. If a 20-year-old had this reaction it would be over the top, but it's par for the course for a middle-school child.

Peer Group

As Zara's case illustrates, the peer group assumes a pivotal role in the life of the middle-school child, much more so than for the younger child. Middle school is the time when peer relationships start to take on new meaning. What peers think, do, and say—the clothes they wear, the music they listen to, the books they read, the movies they like—shapes how kids see and feel about themselves. For young adolescents, the peer group becomes a central force in life. What's happening with the group has a profound impact on how kids see the world, and this leads us to the issue of peer pressure.

When we think of peer pressure, we often think of kids compelling each other to do things that are risky or potentially dangerous, such as using drugs or drinking. In an effort to combat the lure of the peer group, we encourage kids to stand up to this kind of pressure and to think for themselves. As a way of bringing this point home, parents ask their children, *if someone told you to jump off a cliff, would you do it?* And the kids I've worked with get this point, and they will parrot back to adults exactly what they want to hear—*of course I wouldn't do anything like that*, perhaps even believing it. But studies of the adolescent brain indicate that it functions differently alone than when it's surrounded by other adolescent brains, and this has a major impact on the ability to make good decisions independent of friends' bad ones.

Let's return to Carrie for a moment—the girl ashamed of her friend's shoes—and see how this might play out. Carrie and Gail eventually arrived at the mall and met up with their other friends. By this time Carrie had been sitting on her shame and embarrassment about Gail's shoes for a while, and she'd worked up a good deal of irritation at Gail for subjecting her to these feelings. Carrie, like all young adolescents, didn't have much perspective on her feelings and didn't understand that Gail's shoes had very little to do with them. Carrie needed to deal with her feelings—they were consuming her—so the moment she was alone with another friend (presumably one with acceptable shoes) Carrie let 'er rip.

"Can you even believe her?" Carrie said out of earshot of Gail *"Look at what she's wearing!* Those shoes are such a joke!"

Her friend nodded knowingly at Carrie. "That's what she's like," the girl replied. "She's such an idiot—like, who would ever do that?"

"I know," Carrie replied. "She's so selfish. I think we should ignore her for the rest of the day. That'll teach her a lesson." The friend nodded again, although she was a little hesitant about shunning Gail in this manner. "Do you think we should? I mean, really?"

"Totally!" Carrie urged. "Seriously, or whatever—do what you want to do. But I am *so* over her right now. I can't deal with it."

"Okay," the friend agreed, not wanting to upset Carrie any further.

All of a sudden, we've got some social exclusion going on. Of course, this seems ridiculous to us, but only if we don't understand the process underlying the actions. Let's add digital technology to this scenario and imagine that the shunning got played out via text message or on Facebook. If Carrie posted her comments, then more people would have been included in the process of Gail's derision and social exclusion, and if Carrie then rallied some friends to comment, then a whole group of kids could be accused of cyberbullying, and all because of a pair of shoes.

Carrie made some poor choices, this is true, but at no time was it her primary goal to target or harass her friend. Admittedly she was not kind to her friend, but none of Carrie's behavior was motivated by the desire to hurt her. In fact, her behavior was entirely about her own feelings of insecurity, and this insecurity is virtually unavoidable during early adolescence. This explains why middle-school children report seeing bullying, as it is currently defined, everywhere.

For middle-school children, feelings of self-consciousness and sensitivity ensure that they will feel victimized at almost every turn. Ask Carrie about her situation and she would claim that it was all Gail's doing. Of course, this line of reasoning doesn't make sense but this is how the emotional and sensitive teenage brain works.

Development and Zero Tolerance

When we consider how to respond to childhood aggression, all of the above aspects of childhood development must get factored in for us to respond effectively. Zero Tolerance approaches don't allow us do this. Instead, by holding children accountable to standards of behavior that they cannot meet, or that are developmentally inappropriate, Zero Tolerance sets children up to fail.

I recently spoke with a mother whose school district had instituted a tough Zero Tolerance anti-bullying policy at the beginning of the school year. Initially, the mother thought this was a good idea. She had never dealt with bullying herself, but she wanted to make sure her four-year-old daughter was safe, and she assumed the school's policy was a step in the right direction. Until her daughter was the one accused of bullying.

One day at recess, an older child observed the girl shoving sand into the mouth of another child. The school did nothing about the incident even though they too had observed it, since they knew it was just a case of four-year-olds playing together—sometimes sand ends up in the wrong place. Plus, no one got hurt. Nevertheless, the incident got reported to the father of the affected child and he wrote a letter to the school, accusing them of not handling the bullying problem that was occurring on the play-ground. All of a sudden, because the charge of bullying had been made, the school had to activate their anti-bullying protocol. They did not have the option of not doing so because the district was required to respond to every incident of supposed bullying, whether they agreed with it or not. As a result, the mother of the accused child had to come into school to meet with the administration, attend an anti-bullying workshop, and the incident was reported in the student's "file." And why? Because the Zero Tolerance machine had been switched on.

I hear about cases like this all the time. Once bullying is declared, the Zero Tolerance boom is lowered, and the nuances and vagaries of child-hood are ignored in the service of supposedly keeping children safe. This means children can't win or be kept safe in any true sense of the word. With Zero Tolerance, the problem at hand is defined in an ironclad way, which means solutions are neither creative nor suited to fit the situation. By disregarding who children really are, and what they're capable of, Zero

Tolerance thinking assumes they are something that they're not. Rather than setting the bar too high for children, Zero Tolerance sets it too low for adults. It lets adults off the hook for having to think deeply about children's problems and having to spend time in finding solutions.

Digital Technology and Zero Tolerance

Children haven't changed, but the times have, and nothing has changed more in the last generation than technology. Technology is rapidly transforming childhood, particularly regarding the phenomenon we term bullying. In fact, technology not only heightens our awareness of what happens between kids, it also shapes and determines it to some degree. Children now have a public forum in which to misbehave, and adults can see what they're doing. This has created the perception that what is happening is worse than in previous generations but it isn't—it's just gone viral.

Let's circle back to the 14-year-old boy who posted a mean comment about a girl on Facebook and got choked as a result. The mother in question didn't choke the boy because he said something mean about her daughter. She choked him because he posted something that she was able to read again and again and again. Each time she read the post, the boy's misdeeds increased exponentially in her mind, and no doubt she used this perception to justify her subsequent actions. Would this same boy have repeatedly hurled insults at this woman in person? Probably not, but this is what his actions felt like to her. It seemed as though he was in her face, and the insults kept on coming; he just wouldn't go away. The woman admitted as much when she said the boy was never going to stop, and this was true *from a digital perspective*. Thanks to digital technology, she could relive his mistake for the rest of her life, if she chose to.

Parents and schools spend lots of energy trying to help children understand how their digital behavior can have this kind of lasting and devastating effect on others (and this is a good thing), but I know plenty of adults who become irate when kids don't heed their warnings. Given what we know about the developing brain, it's unreasonable to think that kids can employ good judgment or impulse control just because they are up against a force that won't allow them to forget their mistakes. Telling kids that technology will magnify their mistakes won't accelerate their development any more than telling them to grow faster will. Growing up doesn't work this way; it takes time. However, every moment lived online lingers in eternity, and adults must acknowledge this as we figure out how to help children deal with their mistakes. From this generation forward, kids will continue to make all the same blunders as usual, but now these mistakes will be captured by technology and frozen in time, and will follow them indefinitely.

Adults understand how this affects our approaches to children and their social mistakes. We must factor in how our repeated exposure to their misdeeds can blow our reactions way out of proportion. Viewing their mistakes again and again makes us feel angrier and more frustrated with them, but it doesn't make the mistake itself any worse, and we owe it to children to consider this point well. If we don't, we are setting them up to fail yet again.

A fellow school counselor worked with a father whose 13-year-old son went through a rough patch with a classmate during 5th grade. The classmate said some harsh things to the boy in an e-mail—including that he hated him, which upset the boy very much. Over the next two years, the father frequently referred to this e-mail whenever his son mentioned the other boy, and in this way, the classmate was still paying for his sins years after the fact. The father's anger was kept alive and refreshed whenever he reread the e-mail, and to him the boy's words were concrete and permanent. When someone suggested the father discard (or at least, disregard) the e-mail, he took offense. To him, the e-mail was solid and irrefutable evidence that his son had suffered at the hands of another, and it was his job as a father to remember it.

I see this kind of reaction from parents all the time. Because our generation didn't have to deal with situations like this we don't have a reference point. To us, saying *I hate you* in an e-mail seems unbelievably harsh and to have something like this down in writing makes it all the more serious in adult eyes. However, if someone hated us when we were young, chances are the sentiment wasn't written down, so we didn't have a constant reminder of it. But now, with texting and tweeting and Facebook, an ill-advised comment is now in the public domain forever, and our cultural reaction to it is has ballooned with the medium, accounting for much of our nation's current hysteria around bullying. But we can't hold children responsible for the way their mistakes reverberate due to technology. We must afford them the same courtesy we were afforded as children, which is the luxury of forgetting.

Consider what our own lives would look like if we were still being held accountable for mistakes we made in the 5th grade. It's just not fair. For those who think the consequences for bullying aren't harsh enough, I offer this kind of memorializing of childhood as proof that the consequences are often way too harsh.

In addition, children are set up to fail if we don't pay greater attention to how they can bounce back from exposure to painful interactions. Digital technology is here to stay, and even though kids can't grow up faster because of it, adults can make a concerted effort to teach them how to deal with it. As I mentioned, most of our efforts focus on how kids should be responsible for what they say online. This is fine, but what we also must do is make sure kids can handle the stuff that upsets them, and be realistic that, as long as they communicate in this way, there's going to be a lot of frustration. We are setting kids up to fail when we don't prepare them for dealing with the unseemly realities of technology. Sure, it would be preferable to never have someone post something nasty about you on Facebook, but, more to the point, how are you going to deal with it if and when they do? As long as the focus remains on the kid who made the stupid remark, then the kid who was on the receiving end of the remark, and hasn't been taught how to deal with it, is being set up to fail.

Zero Tolerance and the Bystander

A final way in which Zero Tolerance sets children up to fail is with the concept of the bystander in the bully-victim scenario. One anti-bullying education website claims, "Bystanders are as guilty as bullies."[21] But who, exactly, is the bystander, and why are they being saddled with all this responsibility?

The bystander is a relatively new concept when it comes to childhood aggression and it is an interesting character in the bully drama. Bystanders don't ally with bullies per se but they also, by definition, don't

---

21. Soren Bennick Productions, www.sorenbennick.com/power_of_one. html.

come to the rescue of victims, presumably when they could/should. A bystander to bullying is different than a bystander to other situations, such as a train wreck, for instance. A bystander to a train wreck watches from the sidelines but doesn't have any power or responsibility to stop the train; this bystander doesn't participate in the wreck. A bully bystander, on the other hand, participates in the action by virtue of his/her proximity to and awareness of it.

In general usage, the term bystander is neutral until we add a qualifier to it such as "innocent," but not in our current bullying rhetoric. Bystanders are never innocent. To be a bully bystander is to be a full-fledged accessory to the crime. The presumption is that not only *could* bystanders come to the rescue in the bully drama, but that they *should* come to the rescue, and when they don't (and they don't, otherwise they wouldn't be bystanders) they have participated in bullying to an equal degree as the supposed bully.

This is troubling for a number of reasons, the first being how simplistically it renders interactions between children. The bully is over here, the victim is over there—both are clearly identifiable, of course—and the bystander is over there. Everyone plays a clearly defined part in the bully drama and everyone understands their role: no complexity, no nuance, no room for interpretation. Now, with the inclusion of the bystander, every kid *must* play a part—you can't just be standing around twiddling your thumbs, watching your peers interact with each other. No, if you see what's going on, even if you don't really understand it, you are involved, no matter what. You are a *bystander*, and you are *as guilty as a bully*. Even if you're just five, or eight, or 12 years old, you're *guilty*? Yes, this is what being a bystander now means to our children.

In its desire to help kids help each other, the anti-bullying movement is conflating responsibility with empathy and compassion. Of course we want children to be sensitive to the needs of their friends, especially if their friends are in pain, but this is very different than telling children that if they don't intervene in situations that are out of their control, then they not only let down their friends but they also betray them as much as the supposed aggressor. This is the most ineffective way to teach kids about helping and empathy because, well, it is not about helping or empathy, not when the situation is painted in such absolute terms. But that's what Zero

Tolerance is and with the inclusion of the guilty bystander in the scenario, everyone now has the weight of the world on his shoulders.

This kind of instruction also flies in the face of the cognitive development of children. How is a seven-year-old supposed to take responsibility for a situation she is presumably not involved in?

Martin's case illustrates the complexity of the so-called bystander position, although Martin wasn't the bystander himself. Martin, age 12, was having trouble at school with his classmate Reggie. Reggie was the kind of kid who went under the adults' radar screens, or so Martin claimed.[22] Reggie constantly said mean things to Martin when teachers weren't around and Martin felt helpless to do anything about it. He also felt abandoned and betrayed by his friends, who heard what Reggie said to Martin and therefore should have done something. Martin had been taught that bystanders were supposed to help, so why weren't his friends helping him when Reggie was being mean to him? To Martin, the situation was clear: Reggie constantly said mean things, Martin felt hurt and bullied, and no one cared.

This was Martin's perspective of the situation, and it was, of course, just one perspective. In fact, Martin's friends had no idea Martin felt hurt by Reggie's comments, plus Reggie made comments about everyone. Some people thought Reggie's comments were funny, others thought they were stupid, and still others didn't care. Martin didn't factor this into his analysis because he was only 12—he couldn't read his friends' minds, just as they couldn't read his. Martin didn't understand that his friends didn't know he wanted their help, and that without their help he felt abandoned by them. Martin made a classic 12-year-old "mistake" when he assumed everyone interpreted the situation the same way he did and from his perspective. But Martin's thinking wasn't mistaken, just as it wasn't a mistake for some of his friends to think Reggie was funny. All the kids, Reggie included, were functioning like 12-year-olds are supposed to function, so they were extremely self-absorbed and saw the situation only from their own perspectives.

---

22. For the record, most kids are savvy enough to keep their meanest and nastiest taunts out of earshot of the adults. Many adults think this skill proves something in and of itself, as though keeping things out of the reach of adults certifies culpability on the kid's part. It doesn't. It proves kids are smart, not bad.

The reality is that 12-year-olds are consumed by thoughts of themselves, and they can't spend too much time in another person's shoes even if they tried. Martin, in his self-absorption, assumed all of his friends were equally as absorbed—with Martin, that is. Martin assumed his friends must have known what he was thinking because it was all-consuming to him. They didn't, however, because they were busy being absorbed with their own problems.

Zero Tolerance Doesn't Work

This doesn't mean Martin or his friends were unsympathetic towards each other, but the truth is they could only comprehend so much about the situation. Martin didn't think he had to tell his friends what he was feeling because it was so painfully evident to him, and Martin's friends had no idea because they were having their own experiences of the situation.

The final reason Zero Tolerance approaches to bullying set kids up to fail is that research indicates they don't work.[23] It is much more effective to implement comprehensive programs aimed at supporting the social emotional health of children than to rely on reactive and simplistic programs. Chapter 4 explores a different approach, one that sets children up for success, not failure.

---

23. Izzy Kalman, *Psychology Today* online, January 2009, www.psychologytoday.com/blog/the-bully-witch-hunt/200901/new-evidence-against-anti-bully-policies.

CHAPTER 4

HELPING CHILDREN: THE GRIT APPROACH

GRIT: The Strategy

Our current approach to childhood aggression doesn't serve anyone. It vilifies children, pits them against adults and each other, and it leaves everyone feeling frustrated and fearful as a result. Even more worrisome is that in the anti-bullying movement's rush to judge and label children, to define bullying in extremely broad terms, and to adopt a Zero Tolerance approach, many of us are left feeling hopeless and powerless. In truth, our current way of thinking has boxed us into a corner and something's got to give, if we want things to improve. We must examine our responses to childhood aggression, and make significant changes in our thinking about it, or we can expect to see the problem grow. Anti-bullying protocols and legislation are inadequate solutions to the problem and, in fact, they are a big part of the problem. Anti-bullying initiatives are throwing fuel onto the fire, and we're all getting burned.

Luckily, there is a better way, and that way is GRIT.

The GRIT approach is a four-part strategy for dealing with childhood aggression. Throughout this chapter, I will introduce and explore each component of GRIT in depth, and provide examples and tips for how to shift our perspective in an effort to help children navigate painful relationships with peers. GRIT gives parents, educators, and adults who care about children the tools necessary to support kids and foster their resilience.

The following is a brief overview of the four-part GRIT approach:

Step 1: Growth Mindset. Right now anti-bullying initiatives deal with problems stemming from childhood aggression with a fixed mindset, and many fears and insecurities about children's safety—and their ability to bounce back from adversity—stem from this frame of mind. The foundation of the GRIT approach is the cultivation of a growth mindset, a perspective that allows us to think flexibly about children's problems and believe in the promise and power of change and resilience. A growth mindset reorients thinking about childhood aggression to promote positivity and hope, and it cultivates the most important qualities needed for raising and guiding children: compassion and patience.

Step 1 of the GRIT approach is to adopt a *growth mindset*.

Step 2: Responding versus Reacting. The worst thing we can do for kids when they have problems with their peers is to react in kind, which means to be emotionally-charged and knee-jerk—to revert to using our own childhood brain by *reacting*. *Responding*, on the other hand, is the ability to tolerate strong and disturbing emotions and situations and taking the time to think things through, which is using the functions of the adult brain. Responding also means being able to consider emotions as important data points about situations, but not necessarily as the most important facts. The essential work of this step is to keep emotions in check and not act on them until we've had a chance to reason through the options.

Step 2 of GRIT is *responding* with patience and thoughtfulness in the face of our children's difficult challenges and bringing the adult brain to bear in emotionally-charged situations.

Step 3: Interventions. Sometimes we must intervene with, or on behalf of, our children. This section will give tips and guidelines for determining how to make the most of an intervention. Interventions are also about discipline. Children need reasonable and fair consequences for their behavior. In this section I will also provide examples of how adults can support children when it comes to their relationships, and how interventions can be arranged so that everyone feels supported.

Step 3 of GRIT is discerning when and how to *intervene*, and what is the appropriate discipline needed in a situation involving childhood aggression.

Step 4: Teach Your Children Well. Currently the method of teaching children about problems with their peers is overwhelmingly reactive, and it's mostly negative. Anti-bullying education sets children up to think their peers are dangerous and either good or bad. Children need much broader education than this, and they also need to be instructed specifically on resilience, seeking support, and managing adversity. This final section is the proverbial lesson plan we should give children in order for them to feel safe and confident in their relationships with others.

Applying GRIT

For the most part, when it comes to solving the problems of childhood aggression, the anti-bullying movement wants and expects children to do the changing. They want children to be nicer to one another and not to make mistakes that cause harm, and when they do make mistakes, anti-bullying advocates want children to transform themselves immediately. Current policies and procedures place enormous expectations on children and yet they ask very little of adults in terms of change and adaptation. Some adults might wonder how we can be better disciplinarians, but most of us are not looking at our own behavior and responses as much as we are scrutinizing the behavior of our children. When it comes to GRIT, this is *our* work and what adults must do to solve the problem. We can no longer just sit back, enact laws and regulations, and hope our children magically transform themselves. Change begins with us.

GRIT provides a new conceptual framework for considering problems that arise from childhood aggression, and it gives us direction on how to proceed.

Recall the woman who choked the 14-year-old boy in the mall. She obviously had no rational plan for dealing with her daughter's situation. Her anger and frustration were her only guides; she didn't consider any other options. The anti-bullying approach to childhood aggression doesn't provide us with many helpful protocols because most anti-bullying programs suggest we follow procedures that keep us feeling victimized and angry. This mother's fear and anxiety were fueled by this attitude, and then her feelings got the better of her. This is precisely what we're trying to teach children *not* to do, but if we want them to develop self-control and thoughtfulness, adults must demonstrate these qualities. The girl who watched her mother choke her classmate learned that it's okay to act on your feelings and lash out impulsively, and that when you do, and when you justify your actions by claiming you've been bullied, you might get off the hook and onto television.

As this case demonstrates, the anti-bullying way of thinking about childhood aggression incites us to rage rather than to resolution. Any conceptual framework that doesn't calm people down before it instructs them to take action isn't going to solve the problem. What this mother needed was a different kind of framework to guide her thinking. She needed GRIT. The four steps of the GRIT approach provide us with four things to consider before we take action. The steps loosely translate into questions to ask ourselves before we proceed in problematic situations. It's a checklist, if you will, to help us make reasoned and effective responses with children. I will flesh out these questions, and the reasons for asking them, throughout this chapter, however I present them in short form here as a way to guide readers into a structured way of thinking about a different and more positive approach to dealing with childhood aggression.

GRIT: The Essential Questions

Question 1: When I am faced with a problem involving childhood aggression, do I approach the situation with a growth mindset?

The following are some things we believe when we adopt a growth mindset:

- Change and growth are possible.
- Failure is an action; it's not part of our identity and it doesn't define who we are; and, this is especially true for children.
- Abilities and skills can be cultivated—children can and do learn when they are taught effectively.
- Children are essentially resilient.
- The learning curve of childhood is steep and long. Children's ages and stages of development must be taken into consideration in understanding any problem.
- There is always hope.

Question 2: Am I responding or reacting to this situation?

The following are things to help determine if we're reacting or responding to a situation involving childhood aggression.

When we *react* we:

- Act impulsively
- Feel out of control and overwhelmed
- Feel scared, helpless, and angry, and we believe our feelings justify our actions, no matter how extreme
- Consider only our own perspective
- Feel isolated and don't seek advice or support
- Turn up the heat

When we *respond* we:

- Think through our options before we act
- Feel in control of our emotions, even when they are very strong
- Consider multiple perspectives
- Consider the welfare of every child involved in the situation before we intervene
- Work collaboratively with others to seek solutions to the problem
- Turn down the heat

Question 3: How should I intervene?

The following are some things to think about before intervening:

- Is the situation unsafe either physically or emotionally?
- What sorts of consequences are appropriate?
- What does the solution to this problem look like?
- Is the solution reasonable and achievable?
- Who can help me consider my options and/or help me to intervene?

Question 4: What do I need to teach and what do the children need to learn?

The following are things to consider about the "lesson plan" we want to teach children:

- What are the specific skills, attitudes, and behaviors they need to master in order to not repeat the mistakes they've made?
- What are we doing to foster resilience in this situation?
- How is our behavior serving as a model for our children?

GRIT: The Frame of Mind

GRIT is not only a strategy for helping kids with their aggression, it's also a frame of mind. GRIT is a necessary attitude to adopt if we want to be truly effective with children. To have grit means to have a firmness of character, an indomitable spirit, and pluck. Cultivating these qualities in ourselves helps support children because grit is ultimately about resilience, and resilience is one of the most important traits we should foster in children. Perhaps the best way to help kids develop resilience is to surround them with resilient adults, or adults who have a sense of grit—thus the GRIT/grit approach is as much about us as it is about children.

GRIT is straightforward and simple, but not necessarily easy. Creating lasting change never is, and if there were a fast and easy method for raising children we would have discovered it long ago. What we're doing now, though, with our anti-bullying initiatives, is attempting to change others, not ourselves. We *can* transform what's happening with our kids, but we have to start with ourselves first.

The 45-year-old woman who choked the 14-year-old boy focused all her efforts on someone who had caused her pain and frustration. As a result, she intervened in a spectacularly ineffective way. She didn't stop to think, to assess the situation, or to manage her feelings; she just reacted, and she reacted poorly. She did this because she felt helpless—the problem as she understood it existed entirely beyond herself, and she didn't understand that she had other options available to her for effecting change.

A lot of us feel this way (although luckily most of us don't act this way), but just because lots of people share this perspective doesn't make it right. That said, we think this way for a reason, in part because the anti-bully movement *wants* us to think this way. In Chapter 1, I reported that one anti-bully website says, "It's always the bully's fault." Declarations such as this contribute to the illusion that we are not responsible for what's happening at the moment, and worse, that we have no power to change things. If this statement were true—if one misbehaving child were always at fault—then we should give up the ghost right now. This way of thinking has stymied us in our current approach to childhood aggression. The good news is that it's not true, and there is plenty we can do to create change, but not as long as we assume it's somebody else's job to do the work (because that person, a child, is at fault). If we continue to look beyond ourselves for the answers, we will continue to struggle to feel better and to support children effectively.

The GRIT approach is about embracing a new way of thinking and responding, and this is where the challenge lies. There are no shortcuts. Unfortunately, shortcuts are what anti-bullying advocates want at the moment, as evidenced by how they currently deal with children. They want easy answers, quick solutions, and they want all of this to happen without us having to look at ourselves in the mirror. That's not GRIT. If we spend some time examining and shifting our thinking, we can work together to create a much healthier atmosphere for children.

THE GRIT APPROACH

Step 1: The Growth Mindset

Mindsets: A Review

A mindset, as you will recall from Chapter 1, is the way we think about something; it is the set of beliefs we hold on any given topic, a conceptual framework, if you will. Our mindset determines to a large degree how flexible we are, how readily we learn from our experiences and embrace challenges, and how quickly we adapt to change. Carol Dweck, the author of *Mindset*, explains there are two mindsets, fixed and growth. As I explained earlier, Bully Language and bully labels both contribute to and are reflective of a fixed mindset. Using such rhetoric to describe childhood aggression means that we see the issue in all-or-nothing terms, and it is from a fixed mindset perspective that we can proclaim, *it's always the bully's fault*, or *bystanders are as guilty as bullies*.

These statements are unilateral and unequivocal, and they point to a way of thinking that leaves little room for encouragement or interpretation or change. A fixed mindset is a view of the world that is set in stone, unyielding, and absolute. It is certainly not about growth, multiple perspectives, or the inevitability of change, and it is a dangerous way for us to think about our children.

Mindsets are particularly important when it comes to children and learning because a fixed mindset can stand in the way of children reaching their potential. It's worth reviewing how a fixed mindset functions before exploring the importance of adopting a growth mindset when it comes to children and aggression.

Let's begin our review by considering the issue of race for a moment. If we claim one race is less intelligent than another, then not only are we applying a stereotype and prejudice, we are also taking a fixed mindset attitude toward intelligence and race. Carol Dweck reports on research that reveals if a child accepts this negative mindset, or is influenced by it, then that child will not perform to her potential when the issue of race is raised (if, for example, that child is exposed to such stereotypic thinking before taking a test, or if she must indicate race on a form before the test).[1]

The same applies to gender, especially to the belief that girls/women aren't as capable as men in science and mathematics. It has been demonstrated that girls' performance in these subjects is affected when a negative stereotype is triggered, which is why educators have tried so hard to break down these beliefs and encourage girls to pursue studies in fields that were historically considered beyond their grasp. Again, such a stereotype is an example of fixed thinking, and those who adopt such a mindset about their abilities will perform (or not perform, as the case may be) to meet the expectation of the negative belief.

As long as a fixed mindset is in place, whether it's within an individual or across culture, the potential and growth of those affected by the mindset is thwarted. This is not news to most people. Most of us are familiar with the concept of negative stereotypes, labels, and their potential for

---

1. Carol, Dweck, *Mindset* (2006), p. 75.

harm, and many of us have no doubt been on the receiving end of a negative stereotype at some point. But this truth seems lost on those who have adopted anti-bullying thinking. When a child is labeled as a bully, it creates as much potential for harm as if that child is called stupid or a racial slur. Regardless of how bad the child's behavior may be, and no matter how angry we are with that child, using the term bully shuts down that child—and everyone around him—in the same way these other labels do. *But what if it's true*, you might say. *What if the kid really is a bad kid? Then isn't the label appropriate?* Not if you want to help that child, and not if you want to foster growth.

Negative labels never serve children, and especially not when learning is the goal. When a girl is told that girls don't do well in math, that girl is set up fail. When a child is called a bully when he misbehaves, the same thing happens. When the girl struggles with math, she needs help; she doesn't need to be told that her poor performance is expected because girls are bad at math. The same should hold true when a child misbehaves. If the goal is to help a child change her behavior and learn something from the situation, then she can't get boxed in with fixed mindset thinking.

I recently spoke with a mother whose 7-year-old son had been called a bully for years. Her son had a strong personality, that was true, but the adults around him thought his personality was a little too strong, and they constantly monitored his behavior and called him out on it, even for things that would have gone under the radar with other children. It was clear both mother and child were weary of all this negative scrutiny, and the mother reported to me that her son had stopped listening when she tried to talk with him about his behavior.

"I know I'm a bad kid!" he would yell, whenever she brought up a situation that was reported to her. The boy was acutely aware of how the adults around him perceived him, and he had become rigid and unresponsive to criticism of his behavior because that criticism was not constructive and never delivered without a negative and inflexible label.

This is an example of a fixed mindset in action, and it's precisely what we want to avoid in children. In this particular case, the boy was not bad, although sometimes he needed consequences for his behavior. He was a strong-willed leader among his peers, but his behavior was well within normal bounds. He also wasn't stupid. Kids pick up on what adults say and think about them, and he knew the adults around him called him a bully. This caused him to shut down when anyone talked to him about his behavior, and understandably so. He picked up on the fact that adults had a fixed mindset about him, and so, at the age of only seven, he had developed a fixed mindset about himself. Some might argue that this was appropriate if indeed his behavior was bad—that bullies should know they are bullies—but even the most ill-behaved child, one whom we think *really* deserves the label of bully, will not benefit from this approach—especially a very young child. Instead of learning something from it or changing their ways, the label will cause children to retreat and resent those around them, just as this young boy did. When it came to modifying his behavior, this child had no motivation to do so because he knew he couldn't win.

When we have a fixed mindset we feel annoyed and exasperated when it comes to children's behavior. For instance, the adults working with this seven-year-old boy were very angry with him. They thought he should be able to change his behavior after one intervention (even though many of his peers supported his antics), and when he didn't, they held it against him and his parents. As this case illustrates, those with anti-bullying thinking no longer have patience for the very long learning curve of childhood, and as a result they expect kids to be perfect. They want children not to hurt each other or to feel great pain because they believe these things will scar them forever. This is fixed mindset thinking in action and it is hurting us, it is hurting children, and nothing is going to change until we change our thinking.

A recent example of this cultural impatience, fueled by the license to label conferred by this fixed mindset, involves the story of an elderly woman bus monitor who was taunted and harassed on the school bus by a group of middle school boys. The incident was captured on video and went viral almost immediately. It caught the attention of the national media and within a few days the bus monitor was making the rounds of the morning talk shows to discuss her encounter with the School Bus Bullies, as the media branded them. One of the TV anchors, a man clearly caught up in the fixed mindset that encourages judgment and self-righteousness, called the boys "narrow-minded monsters." He also said he wished he could reveal their names on the air, presumably as a form of social shaming. In addition, he announced to the audience that he was going to show the video to his own children as an educational tool, to let them know how they shouldn't behave.[2]

This kind of righteous indignation may make for good ratings but it is terrible for children, not to mention how poorly such outbursts reflect on us as a whole. When an anchor of a national television program damns children—none of whom are his, none of whom he has any responsibility for, *none of whom he even knows*—he's abusing his power and bringing shame to his pulpit, or shall we say his *bully pulpit*. This is an example of what happens when a fixed mindset goes wild. In calling the boys narrow minded, the TV anchor did not stop to consider that all middle-school children are narrow minded and do things that, from an adult perspective, are regrettable and stupid *a lot of the time*. That's essentially the definition of the middle school mind, which needs help and guidance to grow, not public castigation and righteous judgment. Another talk show host joined in the verbal stoning and called the boys "such cowards."[3] I'm not even sure how their regrettable behavior demonstrated cowardice, although obviously that doesn't matter, because the talk show host was able to take a potshot at those children with impunity.

The only difference between the kids on that school bus and us (meaning us adults) is that, as children, we didn't have the kind of digital technology that allowed our misbehavior and poor judgment to be immortalized. We have the luxury of being able to forget our worst moments and of not having a news anchor scold us publicly.[4] Not so today's children, whose every mistake can now be broadcast and used as fodder for those who are quick to judge and who see entertainment value

---

2. msnbc.com, June 21, 2012, todayhealth.today.msnbc.msn.com/_news/2012/06/21/12341459-school-bus-bullying-why-middle-school-kids-can-be-so-mean?lite.

3. today.msnbc.com, June 22, 2012, http://video.today.msnbc.msn.com/today/47904789#47904789.

4. Public scolding in this instance would be appropriate and understandable from, let's say, a school principal or someone else directly responsible for the boys' discipline and well-being, but certainly not from someone who was neither directly involved in the situation nor stood to gain personally from it (in this case, either in the form of ratings or feelings of self-satisfaction).

in causing shame to minors. This anchor should feel as ashamed of himself as he wants those boys to feel: ashamed that he couldn't see beyond the rigid and self-aggrandizing thinking that has gotten us to call children monsters in public and feel good about ourselves as a result.

The following day, no doubt fueled by the righteous abandon exhibited by people such as the news anchor, it was reported by another news outlet that some of the boys and their family had received death threats.[5] *Death threats*, and the article reporting this development didn't explain or elaborate on the threats themselves but instead stayed focused on how the elderly bus monitor responded to the fact that death threats had been issued. Even in light of death threats to 12-year-old boys and their families, the story continued to be about the bus monitor.[6]

This is what the fixed mindset looks like when it's applied to childhood aggression. As a culture we seem quick to link adolescent suicides with cases of harassment and yet, when it comes to something such as the above mentioned death threats, we aren't even interested in whether there's a connection between how we think and what's happening around us.

Children are held hostage by this limited thinking and if changes aren't made soon, someone may be foolish enough to see this as permission to kill (it certainly gave one mother permission to choke a child). Considering that I couldn't find any articles written specifically about the death threats, it's not too far-fetched to say that this kind of fixed mindset thinking could give rise to a license to kill.

Ironically, when children make threats against each other on Facebook, for instance, they now might get kicked out of school, but evidently we have different rules for adults, and we can trace it back to the fixed mindset.

---

5. cbsnews.com, June 22, 2022, www.cbsnews.com/8301-505263_162-57458574/karen-kleins-school-bus-bullies-receive-death-threats/

6. From everything I could glean from the reporting of this incident, the woman bus monitor in question seemed to have a very measured and reasonable response to the whole situation (probably because she understood kids). She did not want the boys to be criminally charged (as some people did); she thought community service and an apology would be appropriate consequences, and she did not seem to be seeking attention for her predicament.

The Growth Mindset

Throughout this chapter I will explore what childhood aggression looks like from the standpoint of a growth mindset, which is the cornerstone of the GRIT approach.

A growth mindset, according to psychologist Dweck, "is a starting point for change."[7] If we want to change what's happening with our children we must start by changing our thinking, and to do this we must adopt the concepts of change and growth. As Dweck explains, mindsets aren't something we're born with; they develop over time, and they can be transformed. This is the first, and possibly the most important, tenet of a growth mindset: that change—in ourselves, in others, and in our circumstances—is possible.

Believing in Change, Changing Beliefs

Perhaps the news anchor justified his actions by believing the School Bus Bullies would change as a result of being shamed publicly. I'd like to think his behavior was motivated by a desire to help, although his statements didn't demonstrate he had faith (or any interest) in the boys' capacity to change. In order to have a growth mindset, adults must cultivate the belief that children can change and develop and grow, like seeds in a garden, and, just like seeds, children need to be attended to. We can't just ignore them and hope for the best. Children need attention and guidance and discipline to change, and all of our efforts, if they are to yield the best results, must to be grounded in the belief that change is possible.

One of the themes I see running through the cases of so-called bullying I deal with is a belief that circumstances and people will never change. If we're faced with a dilemma and we believe there's nothing we can do about it, hopelessness sets in, and this just adds to our frustration. In addition, when we feel frustrated and hopeless our patience tends to fly out the window. Having patience helps us cultivate faith and it's also a by-product of faith. The more we cultivate faith, the more patience we develop, and this combination is a potent antidote to stress. Those who are most upset by childhood aggression seem to be the ones who are most

---

7. Carol Dweck, *Mindset* (2006), p. 50.

locked into seeing it from a fixed mindset, which, according to Dweck, "doesn't allow people the luxury of becoming. They have to already be."[8] In my experience, this kind of thinking produces incredible amounts of stress, which just adds to the belief that there's nothing we can do about a situation.

A mindset is our belief system about any topic, such as intelligence, race, or childhood aggression. A fixed mindset limits our ability to think positively and creatively and thus causes stress because positivity and creativity are two of the most important agents of change and stress relievers. When we can't harness these kinds of thoughts we essentially shut down our capacity to solve problems in new and productive ways, which causes even more stress. In this way, a fixed mindset isn't a static state of being; it is a downwards spiral. What we need in order to solve problems effectively is to be caught in an upwards spiral, infused with feelings of hope that change is possible.

Let's imagine that the mother in the mall had an inkling that her daughter's situation could change, and possibly on a number of fronts. This would have helped her to deal with the problem more productively and it would have kept her from reacting so impulsively and violently in the heat of the moment. In order to see the situation clearly, this poor woman needed to calm down more than anything. Having a measure of faith in transformation and growth would have given her some reassurance that things could improve.

What might this have looked like? First, the woman could have had the belief that the boy's behavior toward her daughter might change. Kids this age are changing constantly. As they develop they test boundaries, try on different behavioral hats, and make lots of mistakes in the process. This generally leads them to an increased understanding of themselves, and, as they mature, to modifications in their behavior. Armed with this perspective on adolescent development, the woman might have had hope that the boy would see the error of his ways once they were pointed out to him (in a manner that was aimed at helping him, not shaming or physically hurting him). If this had happened, then he might even have apologized for his behavior and never behaved in the same way again.

---

8. Ibid., p. 25.

Admittedly, it might be too much to expect this woman to have faith in a child whom she believed had hurt her daughter. This might be too great a leap for her to take, so perhaps she could start by cultivating a belief in the change that was possible closer to home. For example, she might cultivate a belief that her daughter could modify her online habits so that she wouldn't be exposed to distressing feedback. Children must learn how to monitor themselves online, and adults need to help kids prepare for and deal with exposure to things that upset them. The woman could make real progress with her daughter in this regard. This might involve limiting or monitoring her daughter's online use while at the same time preparing her for some of the unintended and unpleasant consequences of revealing aspects of herself online, such as receiving nasty comments in response to posted photos (which was the event that triggered the avalanche of distress leading to the boy's assault).

In addition, she could have cultivated a belief that her daughter's feelings about the situation would change (as they inevitably would). All feelings pass—this is the nature of emotions; even strong, scary, negative feelings come to an end—and they pass quicker when we remember this. Understanding this, of course, is a real challenge for adolescents. Their emotions can feel all consuming at times, and sometimes they get so caught up in them that it feels like things will never shift, but parents can provide guidance by holding the perspective that the mood *will* change.

Children must be helped to develop the skills that they haven't yet mastered, such as understanding and regulating their emotions. Just as they need to be fed when they are infants, they need perspective about their feelings when they are adolescents, and they get this from adults who understand that *this too shall pass*. This doesn't mean children's feelings should be ignored or belittled in any way, it just means they need help to keep sight of the bigger picture. A nasty posting on Facebook might feel like the end of the world to a 14-year-old girl but we know it isn't, and it's our job to help kids develop this belief for themselves, or at least to help soothe them until the storm has passed. We do this all the time in other areas: we soothe them when they fail a math test or suffer another kind of disappointment, and it's no different when it comes to their feelings about what a peer has said or done to them. Our job is to help children deal with their reactions, not to immediately seek revenge.

In other words, when a child fails a math test we don't choke the math teacher in order to solve the problem.

Fortunately, we can also seek help when we feel overwhelmed, so we don't have to go it alone. We should believe in the power of our community to give us support and perspective. For example, this woman reported that she choked the boy in the mall because her daughter expressed an intention to hurt herself in response to the boy's behavior. This was the tipping point for her, and she offered this as justification for her actions against the boy. But rather than being an acceptable excuse for what she did, her rationale instead provided evidence that she didn't believe the situation could change from within, or that she had any power to create a healthy solution.

Following fixed mindset logic, the woman believed her daughter's problems would be solved if the boy suffered, too. Compelling as this idea seems when we're in the grip of pain, this simply isn't how healing works; she could have killed the boy and still not improved her daughter's situation. A far better strategy for everyone involved would have been to seek professional help for her daughter, from someone such as a counselor, pediatrician, or spiritual leader. This would have been a step on the growth mindset path.

Would this have been easy? No, not coming from a fixed mindset. Approaching the situation with a growth mindset would have required some real work on the mother's part, but the payoffs would have been significant had she taken this path. If she believed the situation *could* change, and that she could effect this change, there could have been positive outcomes.

For example, perhaps she could have helped her daughter examine and modify her online habits in an effort to limit exposure to hurtful stimuli. By reaching out for technological help (from a local librarian, let's say), she could have learned how to block certain people from interacting with her daughter online. From a counselor, the daughter could have learned not to take things that are said online too personally. She also might have learned how to deal with her overwhelming feelings (something most adolescents could use help with), and this would have given her insight about how she reacts to things—what kinds of things trigger her feelings of helplessness—and the skills she needed to manage her feelings without resorting to thoughts of self-harm. The daughter would have been much less likely to face a similar situation in the future because she would have learned something from working through the problem the first time around, and she would have been transformed by the experience.

In order for any of this change to happen, both mother and daughter would have had to actively engage in this process for it to yield results. Like physical exercise, the work would have gotten easier over time. It's not an instant fix, but change is guaranteed when we take small steps every day. I like comparing the process of changing mindsets to exercise because everyone can relate to facing a physical challenge, whether it's climbing a mountain or running a race or even walking around the block when fatigued. Take the challenge of running a marathon. The prospect can seem daunting at the outset but no one runs a marathon on the first day of practice. Maybe we begin with a short jog, but it's a start, and it heads us in the right direction, and just because our workouts seem hard at times—and just because our muscles fatigue—that doesn't mean we're doing the wrong thing. As we continue with our training we get into shape and soon our work produces bigger gains for less effort. If we jog regularly, then one day we can do five miles with ease, and the idea of completing a marathon is no longer out of reach.

This is the same process that occurs when we change our mindset from fixed to growth. It takes effort and dedication but over time the new ways of thinking and behaving come more naturally and, if we stick with it, we can achieve our goals without undo effort. One of the hallmarks of the growth mindset is recognizing the value of this kind of effort. Those with fixed mindsets, on the other hand, believe they have to be perfect already and that if they have to work hard then there's something wrong with them. I suspect this mother felt this way, which is why she resorted to violence: choking the boy seemed easier than having to think things through. I have sympathy for her feelings of frustration and fear but her solution to the problem didn't work for anybody, and she was lucky she didn't cause lasting damage.

To repeat, changing beliefs doesn't happen overnight. It's a gradual process, and it's not as simple as just replacing one set of beliefs with another. As Carol Dweck explains, it's more akin to slowly adding a new perspective to an existing one, and nurturing this new outlook so that one day it overshadows the preexisting one. We may have moments when the old fixed mindset rears its ugly head—especially when children are in distress—but our burgeoning growth mindset, if we attend to it, will help get us back on course once again.

In addition, Dweck explains that core beliefs aren't just ideas we have on any given subject, they determine our life. That's right, *they determine our life*. This concept may seem irrelevant to the parent of a suffering child but Dweck's statement is absolutely true, and the good news is that we can choose our beliefs—we have control over how and what we think, which means we have a lot of control over our lives.

For instance, consider the middle school boys who misbehaved on the school bus. We can think of them as *School Bus Bullies* or *narrow-minded monsters* or *cowards*, as the media did, or we can think of them as 12-year-old boys who misbehaved on a school bus and need some serious guidance and consequences for their behavior. This is not just a question of semantics. One approach leads to death threats and the other one isn't much of a story beyond the boys' own community. We can't ignore the fact that our beliefs have serious consequences and these consequences have a profound impact on kids.

So, which beliefs should we adopt when it comes to our children? The ones that make us even angrier with them and lead us to believe that death threats are acceptable, or the ones that bring perspective to the situation and keep us invested in helping the kids who need our help the most?

Up until now the anti-bully movement has presented the issue of childhood aggression as though there's only one right way to think about it. They proclaim their beliefs with such certainty and confidence that we have to look long and hard before we see some of the problems with the underlying assumptions. The problems are there and they are very troubling, and they begin with the belief that the current mindset and perspective on the issue is beyond reproach—that it's *the truth, the whole truth, and nothing but the truth*. How else could someone declare so confidently to the nation that a group of 7th graders are narrow-minded monsters unless he believed he had a corner on the truth? The authority with which anti-bullying advocates (and the media) have defined the issue of childhood aggression, and framed the debate on it, leaves little room for considering it from other perspectives, but there *are* other ways to think about it—the bullying truth isn't the whole truth, by any stretch—and the growth mindset provides us with another way of seeing things.

No More Bully Language and Labels

This leads me to the simplest method we have for creating this shift from a fixed to a growth mindset. We must stop using the bully rhetoric. We must stop calling kids bullies, stop calling kids simple-minded monsters, and stop casting children as the enemy. This aspect of GRIT is truly easy to implement, and we can do it immediately. It doesn't take any self-analysis or soul searching to make this change; it doesn't require any special support or professional guidance. It just takes an understanding that the core beliefs expressed by this kind of language are extremely limiting and damaging. At best, they keep us fixed, frustrated and stuck and, at worst, they escalate situations in a way that makes them harder to deal with and solve.

If we discard this language we must replace it with something else and we have to do more than just transpose words. It isn't enough for us to use the term *harasser,* let's say, instead of bully. We have to get beyond all labels and start looking instead at behavior.

It's About Behavior, Not Character

With a growth mindset the focus is on children's behavior, not on their characters. Recall from Chapter 1 that Carol Dweck's research found that labeling children *smart* actually hampered them. Kids who think things like intelligence are fixed—and they get this idea from labels such as *smart* and *stupid*—can develop a fear of taking risks and failure. This makes them less able to utilize whatever talents they have because they dread making mistakes and not living up to the expectation that they're smart. Children who focus on effort, on the other hand, and who recognize effort as the key to their success, feel comfortable taking risks and aren't devastated by failure—to them, making mistakes is just part of the process of development and it's something to learn from.

Considering the problems that result from using a "positive" label such as *smart,* think how fixed and stuck and fearful children become when they hear terms such as *bully*, *victim*, etc., applied to them. What they need to hear in order to develop a growth mindset—and in order to listen and be open to changing their behavior—is clear and direct feedback about their actions. They need input about specific behaviors and situations, not judgment about their characters.

Let's go back to the boys on the school bus and see what this scenario might look like from a growth mindset perspective. Remember that the goal is for the children to learn something from this situation. Ideally they can emerge from this experience headed in the right direction, with a belief that they can do better next time, and with clarity about what is expected of them.

The goal is for children to understand that *we* have confidence in them, and in order to achieve this we should proceed in the same way we would when children fail in any other aspect of their lives. If they fail a math test, calling them stupid or making them sit in the corner with a dunce cap on doesn't help: they need accurate feedback about their behavior and appropriate consequences. They need to know what they did wrong, understand expectations for going forward, and have faith that they can do better next time, if they work at it.

As for the School Bus Bullies, this process would start by *not* calling them School Bus Bullies or broadcasting this judgment all over the place. Instead, in describing the situation, they could be seen as four 7th grade boys on the school bus who behaved well below expectations. Specifically, they need to understand that their behavior was disruptive and in violation of school rules, and why. The boys would need to be informed that:

- Calling the bus monitor names and taunting her was rude, disrespectful, unruly, and in violation of rules of good comportment.

- This behavior made the bus ride unsafe (not to mention miserable) for everyone.

- This kind of behavior is completely unacceptable and will not be tolerated.

- We know you can behave better than this, and we expect you to do better in the future.

- This would then be followed by consequences suited to the bad behavior. Consequences might include:
  - *Suspension from school*
  - *Suspension from riding the school bus*
  - *After-school or in-school detentions*
  - *An apology to the bus monitor and perhaps to the rest of the students on the bus*
  - *Writing an essay on accidents caused by driver distractions*
  - *Any other consequences that seem appropriate given the culture of the school*

All of this would be followed by a clear explanation of future consequences should the behavior happen again.

Accurate Mirroring

An important aspect of the growth mindset is mirroring. *Mirroring* is a process of reflecting back to children what we see, and *accurate* mirroring is a process of providing children with a realistic view of their behavior, as in the example above. This is how true self-esteem develops: kids learn how to trust themselves and others by getting realistic feedback about how they behave. It also is a process that helps children develop resilience. Conversely, *inaccurate* mirroring involves telling children that everything they do is special (or terrible). When the slant is toward specialness, inaccurate mirroring is about giving everyone a trophy. When everyone gets a trophy, nobody wins, and nobody feels like they've accomplished anything. When the slant is toward terribleness, inaccurate mirroring is about never being good enough, no matter how hard you try. Inaccurate mirroring in either direction erodes self-esteem and resilience because it leads children to believe that effort doesn't matter.

In order to develop resilience, children need to know that effort *does* matter. To this end, accurate mirroring involves praising a child for his effort when he gets an A on a test, or giving him serious consequences when he taunts the school bus monitor. The set of behaviors that resulted in the A is praiseworthy, whereas the set of behaviors that resulted in the school bus monitored getting heckled is not. This might be the same child in different scenarios with different but *accurate* mirroring in each case.

Some of the most insecure and disturbed children I know are the ones who get inaccurate mirroring. These are the kids who can do either no wrong or no right in their parents' eyes; it's as if nobody sees them clearly at all. Children need to know that their behavior means something, and in order to mean something the feedback they receive from the outside world must match what they're doing: it can't be uniform. Getting the same feedback about everything is meaningless. As I say to parents to make this point: not every finger painting warrants a place on the refrigerator.

This can be hard for parents to hear in our self-esteem obsessed world. Some mistakenly believe that they must give their children positive feedback at all times in order to make them to feel loved. This couldn't be further from the truth. What children need in order to feel loved and resilient is *accurate* feedback, be it positive or negative. Accurate mirroring is also the most effective way to help children feel safe. Children know they are safe when they're surrounded by people who will tell them the truth, which is what accurate feedback is all about—the truth. The girl whose mother choked the boy needed to hear that, although she felt awful at the time, she was going to get through her tough experience, that it wasn't the end of the world. As this example demonstrates, accurate mirroring doesn't mean we parrot back to children what they're giving out—in this case a good dose of adolescent angst—it means we provide children with a realistic view of the big picture and their place in it.

I worked with one child who was so accustomed to getting constant and uniformly positive feedback that she didn't have a sense of who she was without it. When she was 7 years old, she was invited to a classmate's birthday party. She was excited because there would be a trampoline at the party, and she loved trampolines. However, soon after she arrived she became sullen and refused to participate. When her mother picked her up to go home, she asked about the party.

"I hated it!" the girl said.

"Why?" her mother asked.

"Because nobody watched me jump."

This girl was so accustomed to being given positive feedback at every turn that when it came time for her to do something on her own—something she liked to do and was excited about doing—she couldn't enjoy herself because she wasn't the focus of someone's unwavering, adoring gaze. As is typical for kids with histories such as hers, when she wasn't the object of someone's undivided attention she didn't want to make an effort, even when the goal was to have fun.

The parents who mirror their children in this way generally do so for one of two reasons. Either this is how they were raised, which was the case with Trampoline Mom, or this is how they *wish* they had been raised. Most of us can look back to our own childhoods and recall times when our parents let us down; they weren't there for that soccer game, or didn't pay attention to our science fair project, or shouted at us for doing something wrong. Now we assume that many of our problems stem from these failures on our parents' parts. *If only I'd gotten more attention*, we think. *Then I'd feel better about myself.* This might be true, but only if the attention we had received back then had been *accurate* mirroring, not some ceaseless stream of candy-coated adoration. Often such retroactive fantasies about childhood are the psychological equivalent of wishing we'd been fed candy all day long. Some of us equate being praised and adored with feeling good about ourselves, but this isn't how self-esteem or resilience develop. Having someone praise our every move on the metaphoric trampoline wouldn't have helped us feel good about ourselves, regardless of how much we think we would have liked it at the time.

Children need accurate mirroring in all aspects of their lives, but this doesn't mean we have to, or should, give them feedback about *everything* they do. This doesn't build resilience either. Accurate mirroring means providing an honest accounting of how they behave, and sometimes this means not paying much attention to them at all. The thought of not paying attention to children can strike terror in the hearts of parents such as Trampoline Mom. They worry their children will suffer without constant positivity, but they also fear that their children won't love them if they don't feed them a daily diet of adoration. Every parent wants their children to love them, but many parents also want their children to *like* them, and parents for whom this is true are often willing to sacrifice accurate mirroring in the pursuit of being liked. When this is the case, the tables are turned and the child functions as a mirror for the parent, and this usually ends in disaster.

In order to mirror children accurately, parents must do away with the fantasy that their children should like them, or that children liking them is a good gauge of their parenting. It's true that sometimes children give us lovely feedback and make us feel great about ourselves, but it's equally true that they can make us feel lousy. Parents need to be able to tolerate feeling lousy if they want to provide children with accurate mirroring and the foundation for true self-esteem and resilience.

In the end, when children behave poorly they need to be mirrored accurately and learn that their behavior is off the mark. When children are hurt they must also must be mirrored accurately, and learn that they will be okay despite these hardship. In this way they develop resilience.

Essential Questions for Maintaining a Growth Mindset

In order to foster a growth mindset when dealing with childhood aggression, we should ask ourselves questions that will prompt us to stay headed in the growth direction, questions such as:

- Am I approaching this situation with the attitude that growth and change are possible?
- Am I treating failure as though it's an action and not a reflection of character?
- Do I believe that skills can be taught and cultivated?
- Am I mindful that children are resilient?
- Do I have patience in this situation?
- Am I hopeful?

Answering *yes* to the above questions let's us know that we're approaching a situation with a growth mindset.

Step 2: Responding versus Reacting

The next step on the GRIT path to dealing with childhood aggression is *responding versus reacting*, which concerns our tone and attitude. If the growth mindset is about our thoughts and conceptual framework, then *reacting versus responding* is about our feelings and emotional state.

Responding is about being thoughtful, cool-headed, and patient.

Reacting is about being overly emotional, hot-headed, and impatient. When I talk to parents and teachers about dealing with problematic situations with children, there are metaphors I use to explain the differences between responding and reacting. The first one is about heat.

Turning the Heat Up/Turning the Heat Down

The question I ask myself most often when I deal with kids who are having difficulties with one another is *are our practices turning the heat up or down?* By this I mean, are our plans of action, and the way we're thinking about the situation, serving to get us more upset and agitated, or are they calming us down? There may be no more important question than this as we proceed with our children, because turning the heat up inevitably entrenches us deeper into the problem—no matter how much the particular response may hold the promise of resolution—whereas turning the heat down just as inevitably leads toward a solution.

Heat Up

The heat I'm speaking about is not just metaphoric, although it is certainly that. It's also literal, and we can feel and measure this heat in our bodies. When we turn up the heat we feel it physically: our blood pressure rises and our heart beats faster. We may also sweat and feel panicked. We literally become hot-headed. These are physiological indicators that our nervous system has kicked into its *fight or flight* response mode. When we use Bully Language to talk about childhood aggression we are not calm and relaxed—we become agitated because we are literally turning up the heat in our nervous systems. The labels we use heat us up; the thought that there are dangers lurking out there heats us up; the thought that we're victims heats us up; and the fear that we can't do anything about the situation *really* heats us up.

I have witnessed adults yell at each other while using Bully Language to discuss childhood aggression. Sparks fly around bully labels; they are incendiary, feverish, and explosive. I have seen people in these circumstances try to turn down the heat only to be chastised for seeming to back down, as though retreating from the fire is to deny the seriousness of it. Some like it hot, and the way we talk about childhood aggression is nothing if not hot. But heat doesn't solve problems; it creates them, and adds unnecessary fuel to the fires that are already burning.

The media coverage of childhood aggression has turned our whole society into a bunch of hotheads. Media attention lights a fire under it, and the purpose of this attention is to bring a moth-like audience—that's us—to the flame. The media's primary goal is not to report what's happening, it is to make money, and to do this it has to keep us interested and coming back for more. What keeps an audience coming back for more? Hot and spicy stories: stories about *bullies* and *victims* and *monsters*. That grabs our attention. Let's be honest. The story of four boys misbehaving on a school bus, and saying mean things to the bus monitor, is not worthy of national attention. Who wants to hear about that? Thousands of kids across the nation misbehave in this way on school buses everyday; it's just not news. But *narrow-minded monsters* on a school bus, taunting a *grandmother*, for heaven's sakes, well, now *that's* hot.[9] And when death threats follow, it's a conflagration and we can't possibly tune out because it is so horrible.

When we hear stories such as the School Bus Bullies, we owe it to our children and ourselves to return to the question: are our practices (our rhetoric, our emotional states) turning the heat up or down? We can answer this question by asking ourselves follow-up questions, such as, in the instance of the boys on the bus, is this coverage helping the children and families directly involved? Is it making a contribution to our understanding of this issue in particular or the issue of childhood aggression in general? Can we learn anything useful about how to deal with our own children from how we're considering this incident? Will children in general be better off as a result of how we're thinking about this issue? If our answer to any of the questions above is *no*, then we're turning up the heat.

Some people believe that media exposure in and of itself is important because it alerts us to danger and keeps us apprised of threats, but when it comes to the well-being of our children, we must understand that we owe it to them to consider their problems and challenges without becoming inflamed.

---

9. The fact that the woman at the center of this story was a grandmother figured highly in the media coverage, and it was obviously a ploy to turn up the heat. Who picks on a grandmother, for goodness sake—only a *monster!*

Heat Down

Cooler heads prevail when we turn down the heat. Once we stop seeing red, we start seeing the bigger picture, so turning down the heat is important when we want to solve problems; in fact, it's a must. It's almost impossible to function at our best when we're overheated, and our children deserve our best. Fortunately, we don't have to change our whole way of thinking in the moment to be able to do this; we only have to change our bodies. That's right, a simple shift in our bodies means the difference between cranking the heat up and bringing it down.

The fight-or-flight reaction indicates that the nervous system is heating up. The *relaxation response*, on the other hand, indicates that it's cooling down.[10] The relaxation response is the physiological opposite of the fight-or-flight reaction, and these two aspects of the nervous system can't be activated at the same time. When the relaxation response is turned on, blood pressure and heat rate lowers, agitation decreases, and thoughts stop racing. The relaxation response changes the condition of the body and the state of our mind and vice versa. When we change our thinking we cause a change in our physiological responses. When we actively engage the relaxation response we see the world very differently than when we are in the heat of the fight-or-flight moment.

This is an important point to contemplate: we think very differently depending on which part of the nervous system is activated and, when we think differently, we respond differently. This means the actions we take in the heat of fight-or-flight—when we are agitated and fired up—are likely different than the actions we take when we're cooled down because we think differently depending on the state we're in. The amazing thing is that we have a great deal of control over this process; we can change how our body responds to stimuli, especially disturbing stimuli. We possess the ability to shift our bodies from one physiological state to another, and for our purposes this means we also have the ability to regulate our thoughts.

---

10. *The Relaxation Response*, by Herbert Benson, M.D., (HarperTorch, 1976) provides a clear and comprehensive exploration of the physical mechanism that turns down the heat.

For those unfamiliar with this process, the prospect of being able to change our thinking and modify our responses by changing our bodies may sound nothing short of miraculous (or crazy, depending on your perspective), but it's true. It's so simple that, at first blush, it can sound simple-minded, or anti-intellectual. The solution is to breathe. To change your thoughts and actions, just breathe.

Start by imagining what was going through the mind of the mother who choked the boy in the mall. It's safe to say that she was in the grip of the fight-or-flight response. She was enraged and overheated and furious—her heat was turned *way* up. So let's see what that's like and then figure out how to change it with the breath.

You are the mother of an aggrieved child. You go to the mall to get your mind off things and as you stroll down the promenade you catch sight of the boy who said those nasty things about your daughter on Facebook. Oh my God, you say to yourself. It's him!

Your blood pressure starts to rise as you think about what this monster did to your daughter—posting those awful comments about how she looked. What a bully! you mutter under your breath. You get more and more agitated as you think about how upset your daughter was after reading those comments, and how she cried and cried and cried—non-stop tears—and how she said she never wanted to go back to school again because she just knew everyone thought she was a loser because of what that idiot had said about her. How could he do that to my poor baby?! you say to yourself.

Now you're fuming, as you think about how this idiot ruined your daughter's life. How can this kid be allowed to roam free? you wonder, contemplating the injustice of it all. He's probably at the mall trolling for his next victim! You just can't believe it—there he is, enjoying himself, acting like he doesn't have a care in the world, when your daughter's soul has been crushed. Not on my watch, you say to yourself. I can't stand it anymore. If no else is going to do something about the situation, then I will! You decide you're going to take matters into your own hands because this is just not right.

You're so angry by this point that your hands are sweating and shaking and you can barely breathe and now you can hardly contain yourself. In fact, you can't contain yourself, and you charge towards the boy, and before you know it you've got your hands around his neck and you are choking the living daylights out of him and you don't care who sees you or what anybody thinks or what the law says because this kid has made your daughter's life hell and he deserves what's coming to him, and as you tighten your grip around the kid's neck you think, That's it! This kid's got it coming to him and I'm going to be the one to teach him a lesson that he'll never forget!

This is what happens when the heat is up. If you don't put on the brakes, things can quickly spiral out of control. Note that even though thoughts were floating through the woman's mind, not much thinking was going on. She got swept up in a flurry of raw emotion that fed on itself. She became more and more agitated with every emotional charge until her adrenaline, which coursed through her like a jolt of lightening, propelled her into physical action.

Let's see what a little deep breathing can do to turn down the heat, jumpstart or reorient our thinking, and guide us to solve the problem more effectively.

You're the mother of an aggrieved child. You go to the mall to get your mind off things and as you stroll down the promenade you catch sight of the boy who said those nasty things about your daughter on Facebook. Oh my God, *you say to yourself.* It's him!

Your blood pressure starts to rise as you think about what this monster did to your daughter—posting those awful comments about how she looked. What a bully! *you mutter under your breath. You get more and more agitated and then you remember what your doctor said about breathing, and how you've got to control that blood pressure of yours. You stop walking for a moment and close your eyes—right here in the middle of the mall—and take a slow breath in, and then a slow, deep breath out.*

Deep inhale—pause. Deep exhale—pause.
You feel your heart rate coming down a bit.
Deep inhale—pause. Deep exhale—pause.
You feel a little better now, but when you open your eyes that stupid

kid is still there and your thoughts start to race again. You get angry as you remember how much he hurt your daughter, and how she cried and cried and cried—non-stop tears—and how she said she never wanted to go back to school again because she just knew everyone thought she was a loser because of what that idiot had said about her. How could he do that to my poor baby?! *you say to yourself*

Then you remember to breathe. You stop walking and close your eyes again.

Deep inhale—pause. Deep exhale—pause.

After a moment of breathing slowly you decide to turn around and walk in the other direction—still mindfully inhaling and exhaling— because you know if you see that boy again you will lose your temper. You take another deep inhale—and another deep exhale—and you con- tinue to walk in the other direction.

You can feel how your body is responding to your conscious breath- ing, and it feels better, but then you think about that boy again and what he did to your daughter. Images of taking the matter into your own hands flash through your mind. Just breathe, *you tell yourself as you make your way back to the parking lot.* Just keep it together until you get out of here and you can deal with it later. Just breathe . . .

This second scenario had a very different outcome than the first one. No one lost control and no one got hurt. Deep breathing didn't cause this woman to stop noticing what was right in front of her or from worrying about her daughter, but it did allow her to think clearly and then to make a different decision in the moment, specifically to remove herself from the cause of her distress. Instead of running towards what was upsetting her, she was able to walk away from it, and this is a huge success. By removing herself from the troubling situation, she didn't act out and do something she would later regret (and possibly pay for dearly). By breathing deeply she guaranteed a better outcome for everyone involved.

Obviously, this is speculation, but what is not speculation is how effectively deep breathing works to turn down the heat. Had this woman actually used deep breathing in the moment she would have had different thoughts and as a result made different decisions—that much is certain. She would have maintained her presence of mind rather than blowing her top; she wouldn't have lost her cool.

As the heat about childhood aggression rises around us, with all the incendiary Bully rhetoric and media coverage, we must not take this as permission to turn up our own heat. It doesn't help us or the children we love, and it really doesn't help the children we don't love.

So, before we turn up the heat, we should ask ourselves:

- Are my actions in the service of cooling things down?

- Will my response help everyone feel in control, cool-headed, and calm?

- Am I able to take a moment to breathe deeply and consider my options before I act?

If we respond *yes* to these questions then we know we're on track for turning down the heat, and that we're responding instead of reacting.

Kid Brain/Adult Brain

Another metaphor I use to help explain the difference between reacting and responding is Kid Brain/Adult Brain. As I explained in Chapter 3, child and adolescent brains are very different than the adult brain. Children and teens have not yet mastered many of the cognitive functions that allow them to consistently exercise things such as impulse control or good judgment. They make lots of mistakes as their brains develop, and many of these mistakes are what we now call bullying.

Consider name-calling. Kids do it; we hate it when they do it, but now it's socially acceptable for us to do the same thing to them under the guise of *saying no to bullying*. When adults call children *narrow-minded monsters* and *cowards* in response to their name-calling it's ironic at best; it's not helpful, instructive, or mature. I call this kind of reaction *using the Kid Brain*. When we react to children's bad behavior with the same sort of behavior, we're acting no better than they are, and in fact we're acting a lot worse because *we have a choice*. We have the ability to *not* call someone names when we're angry with them. We have the ability to step back and use those parts of our brains that kids can't because they aren't developed yet. We can exercise the executive functions—such as impulse control and empathy—that our kids haven't yet mastered, and this is what they need from us. They need us to use our Adult Brain.

Kids need us to use our Adult Brain for two main reasons. First, the only way they will develop their own capacity to use their executive functions—their own Adult Brain—is by witnessing us doing so; the brain learns by example and through imitation. Second, children need to feel contained in order to feel safe, and when they see adults behaving like children it makes them feel unsafe. Adults are supposed to behave differently than kids do, and children rely on this. Children trust adults who act like adults; they don't trust adults who act like children. Since one of the goals of the anti-bullying movement is to help children feel safe, the best way for children to feel safe is for the adults around them to use their Adult Brain.

This can be hard for adults to consider when they're dealing with, say, petulant adolescents. At times teenagers can seem so capable and so adult-like that we forget they aren't adults yet. In addition, their behavior can be so destructive and willful that we think, *hey, they really are monsters. Why should I hold back? I'm going to call a spade a spade and see how they like it!* I have felt this way plenty of times in my work with teens, so I understand what the name-slinging news anchor was thinking. But our job is to resist this impulse and respond differently.

We know this intuitively when we deal with really young kids. Let's say a two-year-old has a tantrum, which happens all the time. It wouldn't help for us to have our own tantrum in response; that wouldn't do them or us any good. We might *want* to have a tantrum in reaction to theirs—this makes sense—but such behavior isn't going to get us anywhere. We also aren't surprised when two-year-olds can't control themselves. Again, we may be angry or frustrated that they can't control themselves, but we know it's part of growing up. It's the Kid Brain at work.

We must extend this same courtesy to older children, especially young adolescents, as we teach them how to behave courteously. Calling a 7th grader names is the functional equivalent of having a tantrum in front of a toddler. It's using the Kid Brain to fight the Kid Brain instead of using our Adult Brain to guide the Kid Brain. As a strategy it isn't effective, let alone kind, but even worse, such behavior makes kids feel unsafe. Picture an adult screaming and crying and throwing food in the face of a toddler who is in the middle of a tantrum. How would it make that child feel? Frightened. If the child stopped his tantrum in response it would not be because our tantrum was an effective strategy. It would be because we scared the daylights out of him. If the School Bus Bullies change their behavior in response to having been called names on national television and threatened with death, it won't be because the news anchor employed a helpful approach. It will be because they were terrified and humiliated into submission. The ends simply do not justify the means here, not when the means involve belittling, threatening, and scaring children.

Before we act, we should ask ourselves:

- Are my actions coming from my Adult Brain?
- Are my actions more mature and well-reasoned than those of the children I wish to guide and help?
- Do my intended actions exhibit such skills as impulse control, good judgment, and empathy?
- Will my actions make the children involved feel safe and contained?

When we can answer *yes* to these questions, we know we are using our Adult Brain and responding instead of reacting.

The Three Second Delay

The final metaphor I use to explain the differences between reacting and responding is something called the Three Second Delay. The Three Second Delay is our ability to hold back, just for a moment, before we act. It's our ability to exercise impulse control. In fact, the Three Second Delay *is* impulse control, and we absolutely must have it if we want to set an example for children. When we react, we do so immediately. When we respond, we employ our Three Second Delay.

During this delay (and it could last much longer than three seconds) we have the chance to ask ourselves the question that children can't, which is: am I about to do something I will regret later? Most of us, when we employ our Three Second Delay, can stop ourselves before we do something we will regret. For example, choking a child. If the woman who choked that boy had used her Three Second Delay, she simply wouldn't have choked him. Given the circumstances, in which there was no immediate danger, her Three Second Delay would have pointed her in another direction. She said as much later when she told a reporter, "I wish it would have been another route I had taken."[11] Well, her wish is granted with the Three Second Delay.

Using the Three Second Delay is easy. Count to three before you act. If you have any doubts about the process, count to 10, or 20, it doesn't matter. Just start counting and keep going until you can resist your impulse to do something regrettable. This is the practice of responding at work.

Essential Questions for Responding versus Reacting

All of these practices are about bringing our best selves to bear when we deal with children. They help us to respond mindfully rather than react impulsively. They guide us to thoughtful interventions. It doesn't matter which method works for you; pick one and use it, and before you take action, ask yourself these essential questions:

- Am I responding in a way that is helpful to everyone?
- Am I bringing my highest self to bear in this situation?
- Have I taken the time to make the best decision possible?
- Am I treating others the way I would want to be treated, or the way I would want my own children to be treated?

---

11. ABC News blog, June 4, 2012, news.yahoo.com/blogs/abc-blogs/florida-mom-arrested-choking-14-old-bully-offers-135330347—abc-news-topstories.html.

Step 3: Interventions

Interventions are incredibly important when it comes to childhood aggression. Interventions, which include consequences and discipline, are essential for helping children regulate their behavior, develop compassion and empathy, and learn from their mistakes. Some people assume that because I don't want to label children that I also don't want them to receive consequences for their behavior. This is not the case. Consequences are incredibly important. All of the scenarios in this book demand some sort of consequence because, in every scenario, there is something to be learned and behavior that needs to be shaped.

In this section I will explore interventions with children and what we should keep in mind in order to make our interventions effective. The following are the five main items that we should consider as we prepare to intervene, the first two of which we have already covered.

A. Growth Mindset

B. Responsiveness

C. Safety

D. Discipline

E. Focus on the Solution, Not on the Problem

Safety

Our primary responsibility is to keep children physically and emotionally safe. Assuming that we are approaching an intervention with a growth mindset and an attitude of responsiveness, our next responsibility is to make sure children are out of harm's way. Safety seems like an easy thing to determine, and sometimes it is, but not always. Sometimes it takes a little analysis to figure out what exactly we need to do to establish safe conditions for children.

Let's consider the case of the mother who choked the boy in the mall through the lens of safety and explore what was unsafe about the situation and what needed to happen to reestablish safety.

The encounter in the mall began with a posting on Facebook. The daughter posted a photo of herself on her page and then the boy posted a nasty comment. This got the ball rolling. As a result of the comments, the girl became distraught, and her mother began to fear for her daughter's life when the daughter said she wanted to hurt herself. This is a very serious and unsafe situation; the mother's alarm was warranted. But the unsafe situation was with the girl, not the boy who made the post. By all accounts, he did not pose a physical threat to the girl, nor was he inciting others to harm the girl. As such, the most immediate threat was coming from the girl. She needed to be kept safe from her own feelings of desperation.

Interventions need to begin where the risk of harm is the greatest. In cases such as this, there are a number of ways to proceed depending on the potential for imminent harm.

- Dial 911 and report a psychiatric emergency.
- Take the child to the Emergency Room for a psychiatric evaluation.
- Contact a suicide prevention hotline.
- Contact the child's pediatrician for an evaluation and referral to a mental health professional.
- Contact the school counselor for an appointment and/or referral.
- Contact a spiritual leader for guidance or a referral.

When the mother put her focus on the boy who made the posts instead of on her daughter, she inadvertently made the situation less safe for three reasons. First, she took her attention away from her daughter's potential for self-harm, which needed to be attended to immediately. Second, she risked consequences that would have increased her daughter's distress. How would her daughter have functioned if she, the mom, had gone to jail? In this way, choking the boy destabilized the situation even further and did nothing to reestablish the girl's safety. Finally, even if the boy had repented for his behavior as a result of being choked, the girl may not have felt better as a result. An apology on the boy's part, or his wounding or death, would not have guaranteed her safety because the greatest risk was coming from her, not from him. She was a risk to herself, so dealing with the boy before reestablishing the girl's safety was an ineffective and dangerous course to take.

As for the boys on the bus, the issue of safety is more obvious to identify. Being disruptive on a school bus is dangerous for everyone on the bus, and the risk for grave danger is present if the bus driver becomes distracted. Safety in this situation would mean getting the boys to settle down, which obviously didn't happen, or removing them from the bus, either temporarily or permanently. In a situation where the disruption is egregious, as it was in this case, then a smart move would be to stop the bus in a safe place and contact whoever is empowered to safely escort the boys off the bus, whether that be school personnel, parents, or the police. All other discipline and interventions should come later. The authorities in charge of the situation, such as the driver and the bus monitor, must be empowered to ensure everyone's safety in the moment, and this means being empowered to make decisions such as stopping the bus and seeking help from others. When our concern is to establish safety first, then we must also evaluate the media attention given to these boys as part of the intervention. The death threats that followed prove that the provocative rhetoric did not contribute to the boys' or their families' safety, and on this score such an intervention was decidedly ineffective.

Discipline—The 4 Cs: Clarity, Consequences, Consistency, Change

Once safety is established, children need to be guided by thoughtful and well-intentioned discipline and they need the disciplinary framework to be in place long before they run into the kinds of problems I've been talking about throughout this book. They need structure and boundaries from the very beginning of their lives, and they need to know someone is there to hold them accountable.

Children need boundaries because boundaries make them feel safe. Boundaries can also make them feel rebellious, but that's part of the process of development, too. Sometimes they need to bump up against the rules or regulations in order to learn what's acceptable and what's not, and they need trusted adults to be on the other side of those boundaries, ready and waiting to help guide them in the right direction when they extend themselves beyond their limits.

There is no perfect method for disciplining children, and parents with

more than one child will tell you that each child often needs different consequences at different times. There are, however, some things to keep in
mind that make disciplining easier, and I call them the 4 Cs: clarity, consequences, consistency, and change. The 4 Cs are a recipe for being proactive with children and they help us think through how we will respond
to problematic situations and consider what sorts of consequences make
sense, so that a system is in place when discipline is needed.

Clarity

Children need to know clearly what is expected of them. For instance, if
parents want their children to perform well in school and go on to college, then they need to let them know this early on; they shouldn't wait
until senior year of high school to broach the topic. This doesn't mean
they need to discuss academic performance or college every night at the
dinner table, but it does mean they should weave the topic into the conversation when it presents itself. In this way, a child is not shocked when
it's time to apply. The same holds true for any other expectation we have
of children; for them to be sociable and kind, to think of other people's
needs, to show compassion, to not hurt others, and certainly not to yell
insults at the school bus monitor.

Being clear about expectations is important for two reasons. First,
clear expectations let children know where the boundaries are and, second, such clarity lets them know when and why they will get into trouble.

What do we expect from children? How do we want them to behave?
I suggest parents and educators really think this through, and think about
it specifically, otherwise it will be hard to have clarity. It isn't enough to
want children to be nice and kind, for example; we must consider what
nice and kind behavior looks like and clearly communicate this to them.
Then, when they misbehave, it will be easier to identify the problem.

Children need clarity about their behavior as they approach middle
school in particular, the time when aggressive behaviors run rampant.
Often, a good time to get clear about expectations is when they earn new
privileges or are exposed to new situations. For example, when children
gain access to cell phones and texting (which, of course, can happen long
before middle school), then a conversation about acceptable use is in

order. With social media, and using sites such as Facebook, kids need to know what the rules are and what consequences they can expect if they don't follow the rules.

Many parents feel overwhelmed by having to monitor and regulate things such as digital technology and social media. This is understandable because we are the first generation of parents who have had to deal with this. We can't look back to our own childhood for guidance because we didn't have cell phones or texting or Twitter. Whereas we are in uncharted territory in terms of the means children use, we nevertheless know how children behave and what they're capable of. All of their challenges and struggles are now being played out in the digital world, and we need to determine how to hold children accountable.

I suggest that parents check in with other parents and with their children's schools, and with the school's Parent Teacher Association, for support and guidance. Every parent is struggling to figure this out, so join forces and connect with as many other parents as possible. Find out what the school is teaching children, if anything, about being media savvy, and discover what expectations and boundaries other parents have set. A good rule of thumb is that kids shouldn't have access to social media until they can reasonably manage the consequences. In other words, if parents don't think a child can handle dealing with the downsides of something—such as receiving nasty text messages, or sending them—then it's too early for them to be using the technology.

Children need adults to be in charge. They need rules, and on some level they *want* rules. Without rules and boundaries, children feel the weight of the world on their shoulders, and this is a huge burden. Children need to know what's expected of them, and they need us to be clear about where that boundary is.

Consequences

When it comes to clarity, the thing we need to be most clear about, after expectations, is consequences—specifically, that consequences will follow unacceptable behavior. Creating boundaries for children is just the first step. Consequences let children know that the boundaries are real. Without consequences, expectations are meaningless.

Next, to be effective, consequences must fit the crime, so to speak. When consequences are either too harsh or too lenient—or when children can't see a connection between consequences and their behavior—then consequences aren't very effective For example, the consequence of choking a boy for posting comments on Facebook did not fit the crime well. First, it was much too harsh, not to mention illegal and, second, it didn't necessarily teach the boy anything about his specific behavior and what he needed to do to change. This is what good consequences do: they serve as both punishment and instruction. Choking was punitive but it wasn't instructive.

A more appropriate consequence would have been to take away his online privileges for a time. This consequence is clearly connected to the unacceptable behavior, and time away from the computer and cell phone would have given him the opportunity to appreciate them as privileges, and to think about correcting his offensive behavior.

Parents sometimes roll their eyes when I make suggestions like this, and I understand why. It's hard to function in our world without being connected. But let's face it, we all survived childhood without this technology and so can our kids, at least for a week or two. Children do not need to be in touch with each other or us as much as they think they do, which is precisely why this kind of consequence would be fitting for this kind of behavior. Two weeks of no texting, Facebook, e-mail, etc., would have a big effect on them. They would hate it, and such a consequence would make them think twice about their behavior. And if they need to be online for school, then parents may need to sit with them while they work. It may sound grim, but this is what a good consequence is.

I recently spoke with the mother of a 14-year-old boy who was in this predicament after she caught her son abusing his computer privileges. Her son was posing online as a classmate, and posting things that were very prejudicial and derogatory to the boy he was impersonating. The mother was furious when she discovered this, and became even more so when her son lied about his behavior. She knew she had to make her son understand how serious his transgressions were. She decided he had to apologize to the boy he'd been impersonating and then do without his computer and phone for two weeks. (He was allowed to do homework online at a computer that his parents could see.)

This meant, of course, that she had to be vigilant about enforcing the consequences, and this is where consequences can feel burdensome to parents. I once worked with a mother whose 16-year-old daughter continually violated the rules about driving the family car. She drove with friends in the car when she had been prohibited to do so, broke curfew, was rude to her parents when she wanted to use the car, and left the car a mess. When her mother asked me what she should do to punish her daughter and help change her behavior, I said, "Simple. Take away the car."

"Oh, but that would make everyone's life so hard," she said. "We'd have to drive her everywhere and that would ruin my schedule."

Well, then don't bother having consequences, or sell the car and buy the kid a bus pass. Holding the line around consequences is where parenting gets hard, but, truly, this is the only way discipline works. It's one of the toughest parts of parenting, and I don't know many parents that enjoy it. But this is beside the point. If your child's behavior is out of bounds, then he/she needs consequences, and more often than not a parent (or, if the behavior happened at school, then perhaps a teacher/administrator) is the best person to deliver such consequences.

Consequences also have to fit the particular child. I knew of one 8-year-old boy who constantly got into trouble at school for being aggressive with his classmates. The school gave out consequences but the boy just didn't respond. When a child doesn't respond, it's not necessarily the child's fault; it could be that the consequences need to be reexamined. At this boy's school, the consequence was a conversation with the teacher and the vice principal (and after that, with the parents).

For many children, this would be sufficient, but it wasn't enough for this boy, who came out of these conversations unmoved. After each incident of unacceptable behavior, and after each consequence, the boy remained unchanged, and as a result the adults around him got more and more frustrated. They assumed the boy was immune to consequences. They never once considered that maybe it was *their* consequences that weren't working with the boy, not that *any* consequence wouldn't work. It turns out, this child needed consequences that were more concrete and tangible than just a conversation (such as losing a privilege, for example, like playing with a favorite toy). Once the right consequence was put into place, the boy's behavior started to shift.

On the other end of the spectrum, I know of another boy, this one 11 years old, whose parents issued extremely strict consequences for somewhat minor infractions. The consequences were so strict that the boy lived in a perpetual state of punishment. When his behavior veered off course, he was grounded for a month; at the second offense, it was two months. Whenever he made a misstep, he lost his computer time, TV time, and music—everything he liked to do. It got to the point where eventually his parents had nothing to hold over him; he'd lost everything. His parents couldn't enforce this state of constant deprivation either, so the boy got many of his privileges back—haphazardly and never officially, and never as a result of good behavior—because his parents just couldn't uphold their own standards. This inconsistency meant the boy learned very little from the consequences he received, other than that his bad behavior resulted in more lost privileges but no real change.

Consistency

Consequences must be consistent to be effective. The 11-year-old boy above never received any benefit from the consequences he was given because his parents couldn't enforce them; their words and deeds were not aligned, and therefore their message never got clearly communicated. Inconsistency confuses children, and it lets them know that our words don't mean much. The best-behaved children I know are the ones who have absolute faith in their parents' word; they know it means something. The same goes for the adults who give consequences in schools. If they are consistent, kids will respect them. If they aren't, kids won't.

Change

Change refers to factoring development into discipline. When we take development into consideration, it means we adapt and change our approach to discipline depending on factors such as a child's age and maturity. Change makes consequences challenging because it means *we* also have to change. We must change our approach, our understanding, and our expectations as our children grow and develop.

Considering change is the antithesis of the Zero Tolerance approach because it means we acknowledge that kids at every stage need something slightly different. Luckily, these modifications are much easier to make when we've been clear about our expectations from the start, and as long as we do well with our consistency and consequences, then we can adapt more naturally to our children's changing needs.

Focus on the Solution, Not the Problem

Focusing on the problem is easy; focusing on the solution takes time and maturity. If we are going to help our children deal with their aggression effectively, we *must* focus on the solutions to their challenging behavior and dynamics, not just on the problems. This can be a challenge in our current atmosphere of media sensationalism and repeated exposure to stories, videos, and other information that purport to describe the "bullying epidemic." Problems are newsworthy, solutions aren't. We must pull ourselves away from the din of the media and get down to the business of solving problems.

This aspect of interventions is mostly about our attitude, and if we adopt a growth mindset then we are assured of being solution-focused. A simple way to tell if we're focused on the solution is to ask ourselves if we feel hopeful. Being solution-focused makes us feel hopeful and energized. Being problem-focused makes us feel hopeless, helpless and depressed. To determine our focus all we need to do is to figure out what we're feeling.

Many people stay focused on the problems of childhood aggression because they don't believe a solution is possible, and our Bully Language lends permanence to how we view things, which compounds this belief. When we use bully labels there is no end in sight, because we have no assurance that a *bully* will stop being a *bully*. Labels are the ultimate way to keep ourselves fixated on the problem, and when this is the case, solutions will not only feel out of reach, they will remain out of reach. We have to believe solutions are possible before they can become probable.

I worked with one father who was eager to help his 9-year-old daughter deal with the painful dynamic she was having with a classmate. But he couldn't let go of his belief that the other girl was a bully, and as a result he circled around the problem endlessly, getting nowhere. When I asked him to think about what a solution would look like, he couldn't come up with anything. "She's a bully," he explained. "She's never going to change."

It wasn't until he let go of the label that he was able to believe that something different could happen between the girls. Once he saw beyond the label he could think about solutions, and then he was able to help his daughter think about solutions as well.

Final Thoughts About Interventions

The following are some final things to keep in mind when it comes to interventions.

A. *They're children.* Even an older adolescent still has lots of developing and learning to do. One of the reasons I use the term children so often, even when referring to teenagers, is because we need to remember whom we're dealing with. When we're angry with a child it is different than being angry with an adult. Children are not our equals, and they cannot defend themselves the way we can, and therefore they deserve every benefit of the doubt.

B. *Whatever they did, the behavior/incident in question isn't the whole picture.* It is easy to dismiss and ignore all of the good aspects of a person we're angry with. Recall the celebrity from Chapter 2 who said of the girls who were mean to her, "I've realized girls who do stuff like that will never amount to anything in life. They reach their peak in high school, then that's it—they don't go anywhere."[12] As much as this might be a helpful strategy to move through a painful experience, it's patently untrue. No one is defined by one action, not even the people we are most angry with, and definitely not children. No one is defined by one ill-considered posting on Facebook. We accept this without question when it comes to our own children—we would never think of them as one-dimensional creatures because we see all sides of them—the good, the bad, and the ugly—but this is harder to do when we don't see all sides, and when the one side we see is negative. This doesn't mean we must embrace all aspects of children we're angry with, but it's important to remember that their characters can't be summed up by one experience.

---

12. Bullyville.com.

C. *Whatever we do or say to a child (or to his/her parents) will have a huge impact—they will remember our actions for a long time.* Consider that your actions may be permanent; no one will ever forget that you choked a kid in the mall, least of all that kid and his parents (and their lawyers).

D. *We may or may not be the appropriate person to intervene.* In order for an intervention to be effective it must come from a person with direct authority over the children in question. It's fine for a TV anchor to think he could teach the boys on the bus a lesson by shaming them, but he was neither entrusted with their welfare nor did he have any authority in the situation. All he accomplished by defaming the children in public was to feel self-righteous and blow off steam; he did not intervene effectively with the boys. The school principal, on the other hand, and the boys' parents have the authority and oversight to implement the appropriate consequences. If we want to intervene but don't have the authority or mandate to do so, then the consequences we mete out will probably be neither effective nor appropriate.

E. *Seek advice and support.* Intervening can be difficult. You don't have to go it alone. Talk to professionals, other parents, and friends. When in doubt, reach out.

Essential Questions for Interventions

The following are questions to think about before intervening:

- Is the situation unsafe, either physically or emotionally? If so, what needs to happen specifically to reestablish safety?
- Are the consequences for the behavior clear, consistent, and developmentally appropriate?
- What does the solution to this problem look like?
- Who can help me consider my options and/or help me to intervene?

Step 4: Teach Your Children Well

Social Emotional Learning

The final step of the GRIT approach is teaching children what they need to know about managing their aggression productively and building resilience. This kind of teaching calls for a Social Emotional Learning curriculum that is broad and stretches throughout childhood. It must be as comprehensive and as well considered as any other curriculum; it is not something that can be squeezed into an assembly presentation once a month. Social Emotional Learning should be integrated into existing school programs and taught by people who have training and expertise in this area. They shouldn't be farmed out to the newest or youngest person on the payroll, or handed off to the person who has a little free time. We must focus on social emotional seriously and make it as much of a priority as is our current focus on children's shortcomings. It is unfair and unrealistic to expect children to behave in certain ways if we don't dedicate time to educate them in this realm of their lives.

There are many good SEL resources available (see Resources), so parents and schools can research what is already out there instead of reinventing the wheel. That said, more than other aspects of the curriculum, SEL programs should arise organically from the needs of individual communities. In order to be successful, programs must adapt to and reflect the preexisting values, norms, and tenets of the given community and take into consideration each school and student population's unique circumstances and needs.

For example, school communities differ widely and vary according to size, location (urban, suburban, rural), geography (state and school district), political bent (progressive, conservative, middle of the road), funding source and management structure (public, charter, independent, religious, military), and scope and purpose of program (day school, boarding, special needs, residential treatment). Given such a broad range of school type, it is unrealistic to think every community can or should adopt the same SEL curriculum—the SEL needs of the small independent boarding school will be very different than those of the large, inner-city public school. This is why I will not introduce a specific curriculum here. Instead, the first thing I recommend is that schools and parents work together to create and foster programs that are dedicated to developing the potential of all children in the area of their social-emotional growth.

Resilience

If schools should focus on Social Emotional Learning when it comes to teaching children well, then parents should focus on helping children build resilience. There are many resources on resilience available for parents, especially in the form of websites, books, and articles (see Resources). When parents make resilience a priority, children develop faith in themselves and their ability to handle all kinds of social situations.

Having resilience doesn't prevent children from feeling pain and hardship, but it allows them to face their pain and hardship without feeling undone. More than any other quality, resilience guarantees that children will be able to manage their lives productively. Many parents make happiness a priority for their children because they believe happiness will promote resilience. In fact, it's the other way around. Resilience promotes happiness because resilient children are able to bounce back and take control of their lives; happiness is the by-product.

The great news is that resilience is much easier to promote than happiness because resilience is a skill, not a mood. Skills can be taught, moods can't. Moods can be managed and this is one of the things children need to learn in order to be resilient. If we can place our emphasis on resilience rather than on success and happiness, we will go a long way to ensuring our children will experience success and happiness.

Essential Questions for Teaching Children Well

The following are the essential questions for teaching children well:

- What are the specific skills, attitudes, and behaviors children need to master in order to not repeat the mistakes they've made?
- What are we doing to foster resilience in this situation?
- How is our behavior serving as a model for our children?

We Can Make a Difference

We owe it to children to think about them differently. They are not the enemy. They are not monsters. They are children, and they are no worse than we were. If we keep sight of this fact, and have patience for their mistakes, they will reach their potential.

RESOURCES

Social Emotional Learning Websites

Bullies2Buddies	bullies2buddies.com
Center on the Social and Emotional Foundations for Early Learning	csefel.vanderbilt.edu
Collaborative for Academic, Social, and Emotional Learning	casel.org
Education Week	blogs.edweek.org
Edutopia	edutopia.org/social-emotiona learning
The Responsive Classroom	responsiveclassroom.org

Resilience Websites

American Psychological Association Resilience Guide for Parents and Teachers	apa.org/helpcenter/resilience.aspx
Raising Resilient Children Foundation	raisingresilientkids.com

Books

Dr. Mary Karapetian Alvord, Dr. Bonnie Zucker, Dr. Judy Johnson Grados, *Resilience Builder Program for Children and Adolescents: Enhancing Social Competence and Self-Regulation* (Research Press, 2011).

Robert Brooks, Sam Goldstein, *Raising Resilient Children: Fostering Strength, Hope, and Optimism in Your Child* (McGraw-Hill, 2002).

Carol Dweck, *Mindset: The New Psychology of Success* (Ballantine Books, 2007).

Kenneth Ginsburg, MD., *Building Resilience in Children and Teens: Giving Kids Roots and Wings* (American Academy of Pediatrics, 2011).

Wendy Mogel, *The Blessings of a Skinned Knee* (Penguin, 2001).

Wendy Mogel, *The Blessings of a B Minus* (Scribner, 2010).

Martin Seligman, *The Optimistic Child: A Proven Program to Safeguard Children Against Depression and Build Lifelong Resilience* (Mariner Books, 2007).

ABOUT THE AUTHOR

Susan Eva Porter has worked in schools for 25 years. She began her career at Phillips Exeter Academy, where she launched the school's Health Education program, and since then she has worked with students at every level, from pre-K through graduate school. She has held positions in schools on both the East and West coasts, including counselor, health educator, administrator, trustee, and consultant. Dr. Porter received a bachelor's degree from Brown University, a master's in education from the University of Pennsylvania, a master's in clinical social work from the Smith College School for Social Work, and a Ph.D. in Clinical Psychology from Pacifica Graduate Institute. She currently lives and works in Marin County, California.